Metro Newspaper Journalists in China

This book explores how journalists at local metro papers in a southwestern China metropolis give meaning to their work and how these meanings are shaped by the specific social environment within which these journalists operate. These metro papers provide the bulk of daily news to the general public in China, yet are often understudied compared to the country's Party news outlets. Informed by fieldwork in four metro newspapers, the book puts forward a grounded theory for exploring journalists' occupational culture: the aspiration-frustration-reconciliation framework.

Zhaoxi (Josie) Liu is an Assistant Professor in the Department of Communication at Trinity University, USA.

T0383679

Routledge Focus on Journalism Studies

Metro Newspaper Journalists in China

The Aspiration-Frustration-Reconciliation Framework

Zhaoxi Liu

Routledge
Taylor & Francis Group

LONDON AND NEW YORK

First published 2017 by Routledge

2 Park Square, Milton Park, Abingdon, Oxfordshire OX14 4RN
52 Vanderbilt Avenue, New York, NY 10017

Routledge is an imprint of the Taylor & Francis Group, an informa business

First issued in paperback 2019

Library of Congress Cataloging-in-Publication Data
A catalog record for this book has been requested

ISBN: 978-1-138-67500-1 (hbk)
ISBN: 978-0-367-87860-3 (pbk)

Typeset in Times New Roman
by Apex CoVantage, LLC

To My Parents

Contents

Acknowledgments

I am deeply in debt to Dr. Judy Polumbaum for this volume. She was there since the very inception of the idea of this project and contributed significantly to an earlier version of this volume. Drs. Dan Berkowitz, Frank Durham, Tim Havens, and Wenfang Tang also offered invaluable advice and feedback.

I want to thank my editor, Ms. Felisa Salvago-Keyes, for her faith in the project and wonderful support throughout the course of producing this book. My sincere thanks also go to the two anonymous reviewers for their insightful comments and suggestions, which greatly helped me enhance the manuscript. Drs. Jennifer Henderson and Bill Christ, as well as Professor Sammye Johnson, also helped with the project.

Also, my deep gratitude to all the journalists I encountered in Kunming during my field study. They did not just open their newsrooms to me, but also their hearts. I was deeply touched by their commitment, industriousness, and perseverance. I salute them and wish them the very best.

Finally, I have to thank my family—my parents, sister, husband, and two adorable children—for their tremendous love and constant support. My parents, half the world away, are my strongest supporters and most passionate cheerleaders. This book is dedicated to them. Unfortunately, my father passed away right before the publication of this volume. This book is for him.

Newsrooms of three Kunming metro papers where the field
research for this volume was conducted.

Kunming street.

The army of eBikes in Kunming.

1 Introduction to "Heaven and Hell"

Xiao Zhou[1] is well known among journalists in Kunming as a daring investigative reporter. Other journalists speak of him as legendary and invincible. He describes himself, however, as a hedgehog that turned into a mouse after running through the woods, having lost all his spikes in battle. Born in the 1960s, Xiao has worked in Kunming newspapers for 10 years. He says his ideal is to make journalism do more and serve more people, and he professes to love doing investigative reporting. "Revealing a judge sleeping with underage prostitutes is to make the judiciary and law enforcement fairer. Revealing drawbacks of the political system is in hopes of making the execution of political power cleaner and fairer," he says.

Xiao wants to be "a swordsman" who acts "on behalf of the people," and the stories he and others tell illustrate how boldly he has gone about this mission. Once, he recalls, he had an argument with a propaganda official at the provincial police bureau over a story and the official pointed a gun to his head and threatened to shoot him dead. "I said you go ahead and shoot. If you don't shoot me, I have recorded today's conversation and I will later post it on the Internet. I then returned to the newsroom and saw that police cars already had arrived. Police officers were telling people in the newsroom not to let me touch any computer." I asked if he was afraid. "Of what?" he responded. "[The official was] just trying to scare me" (October 15, 2011).[2]

Like many journalists I met in the course of the current study, Xiao has seen his aspirations come up against hard realities over the years. One night a few years ago, for example, a tipster calling on a news hotline reported that a real estate company had just leveled the ground by Dianchi Lake and buried alive two migrant worker children sleeping in a tent next to the lake. Xiao and a photographer went to cover the story. Afterwards, late that night, their editor invited them to have tea and reminded them that, "We are a market paper," and told them the real estate company had paid 1.3 million yuan of advertisement fee in exchange for the newspaper's silence. The story never ran.

Xiao is dedicated to his job because he wants to "solve people's problems," an aim, however, most of his stories fall short on as far as he is concerned. Xiao once got tips from villagers in his hometown, a rural county west of Kunming, revealing government-supported massive illegal tree felling. He went to investigate the incident and was invited to meet with one of the top local officials. The official begged him to "control the direction of the story" for the sake of his hometown. Xiao ignored the official's plea and the story was published. To his surprise, right before higher authorities were about to punish the local government, main officials related to the misconduct were transferred to other offices, which effectively allowed these officials to escape being held accountable.

Another time, Xiao went undercover at a railroad construction site, posing as a migrant worker to investigate contractors who were embezzling by using lower quality concrete. The resulting story triggered an investigation, and railway authorities ordered some of the construction work to be redone and fined the contractor, but denied use of low-quality concrete and stopped short of investigating the chain of interest that might have linked back to the authorities themselves. Xiao and his editor at the time were furious. "Seeing that the fire is about to burn higher, [they] covered it up," Xiao says.

After all these years and all these stories, he concludes, investigative pieces that expose high-level abuse "are all loud thunder with small rain drops." Each story's publication initially gives him hope, he says. "But eventually, the stories are harmonized and harmonized [a reference to a common official slogan, *hexie*, meaning harmony or "build a harmonious society"], rendered useless" (October 14).

Early in 2011, the editor who had pushed for investigative reporting and strongly supported Xiao left journalism altogether to start his own business of express delivery. Xiao said his best boss ever changed careers out of "despair" (October 14). This editor's successor, a much younger journalist, described his predecessor as "relentless and idealistic about journalism," and concurred that, "He left because he was disappointed about the environment surrounding journalism" (October 18, II).[3]

Xiao himself sounds almost ready to surrender as well. "I have always tried to carry on and would rather die than give up," he says. But he has been tired of suppression and obstruction for economic and political reasons. "I feel like an idiot. There are so many [bad] people out there. As soon as you beat down one devil, another and then another appear." So he, too, is considering a career change, maybe starting his own business. "Go out there to make some money for retirement. Discard ideals completely," he says (October 14).

Many other journalists in the current study express similar ideals about correcting the wrongs of the society and system and making people's lives better. Some speak of upholding social justice and pushing for political change. But like Xiao, these idealistic journalists express deep frustration at the obstructions to their work, ranging from threats to banned stories to having little or no impact even after the stories are published. In short, these Chinese journalists face a huge gap between what they aspire to do and what they can actually accomplish, hence the frustration.

In the eyes of these journalists, Kunming is both heaven and hell for their occupation. They are never short of stories to write about: car accidents, house fires, mysterious bodies, food safety violations, and common people walking into the newsroom with tales of suffering and injustice. At their busiest, journalists have no time for meals or even going to the bathroom. At the same time, they feel limited in the sorts of stories they can actually write. Covering a car crash or suicidal roof jumper is merely doing the daily job, but does not mean much to them. Their aspiration is to be muckrakers, to stop social injustice, and to make a difference. Over and over, they come up against political and economic restraints and end up with enormous frustration.

So why bother? Why do they still stay at the job? Because, as I found through the field research, the journalists managed to, willingly or unwillingly, find some sort of reconciliation to render their job meaningful. For the metro journalists in Kunming, the reconciliation is to help individuals without money or power in small ways. People wronged by authorities, mistreated by public institutions, or simply too poor to take care of themselves may walk into newsrooms to find a sympathetic ear; not uncommonly, an aggrieved person will kneel down in front of a journalist to beg for help. Journalists often do try to help such individuals through writing stories about them, and the stories sometimes result in donations from the public or attention from the authorities—even if it will not have much impact on the broader system. They see this as making small changes when a big change is not feasible.

Together, the aspirations, frustrations, and reconciliations bond these journalists into a professional community with shared ideals, beliefs, norms, practices, and sentiments.

Purpose of the Study

The central question of this project is how these journalists make sense of their work and render their job meaningful. Such is a cultural inquiry of journalism, which has been one of the most fertile fields of journalism studies (Zelizer, 2004). The cultural inquiry conducted in this volume is guided by Carey's (1992) ritual view of communication and Geertz's (1973) theory of culture. For Carey (1992), communication, with journalism as a key component, is a meaning-generating action that maintains shared beliefs (i.e., culture) through time among a group of people. He and Geertz (1973) share the view of culture as a meaning system, as Geertz also maintains that culture is the web of significance that humans themselves spin and suspend themselves on. Culture is an interworked system of construable signs, and it is not a power to which human society phenomena could be causally attributed, but a context within which social phenomena could be "intelligibly, that is, thickly, described" (Geertz, 1973, p. 14). Culture in this sense is not a fixed entity, but contingent upon historical circumstances. Both scholars therefore point out that the essence of cultural inquiries is not an experimental science searching for absolute laws, functions, and effects, but hermeneutics, or interpretive sciences, searching for meaning (Carey, 1992; Geertz, 1973).

"Meaning in this view is not representation but a constituting activity whereby humans interactively endow an elastic though resistant world with enough coherence and order to support their purposes" (Carey, 1992, 85). In this volume, the meaning and the world under investigation are that of a group of journalists—the occupational culture of a particular group of journalists, situated in a broader social context and in connection with other social groups.

It is possible to explore such an occupational culture because these journalists, namely, the metro newspaper journalists in Kunming, work under similar circumstances and share particular values, beliefs, and practices, thus forming a collectivity, much like humans forming a society that is sustained by culture. If culture is the system of meaning that guides human actions and allows them to make sense of their day-to-day behavior, then the occupational culture of journalists could be deemed as the system of meaning that guides journalists' professional action and allows them to make sense of what they do as journalists. Seen through the cultural prism, the world of news becomes "more than just reporters' professional code of actions or the social arrangements of reporters and editors," but "a complex and multidimensional lattice of meanings for all those involved in journalism" (Zelizer, 2004, p. 175). To view journalism as a culture in its own right is to view journalists as a collectivity and community, bound and maintained through patterned behavior and shared meanings, as is human society in general (Carey, 1992; Zelizer, 1997[1993]).

Ultimately, the goal of this volume is to provide a conceptual framework that, devised through a grounded theory approach (Glaser & Strauss, 1967), is useful in understanding the unique culture of a particular group of journalists. The current study demonstrates how, through examining the aspirations, frustrations, and reconciliations of the journalists, the scholar can reveal the shared ideas, practices, and meanings that constitute the occupational culture of a journalist community.

In every society, journalism is different and so are journalists. The aspiration-frustration-reconciliation framework, I believe, can be applied to journalists in different social and cultural settings, as well as different organizations. Depending on the specific type of organization, society, political system, and culture, different groups of journalists can have a different kind of aspiration or ideal for their profession, can face a different kind of frustration due to specific social, political, or cultural forces that obstruct their efforts to realize their professional ideals, and eventually work out a specific type of reconciliation or compromise that fits the broader social environment and allows them to render the job meaningful. In addition, the level of frustration and the need for reconciliation can vary from situation to situation and can become an important indicator of the distinct characteristics of certain groups of journalists.

Journalists in China and the United States, for example, face different hurdles in realizing their professional ideals and have different ways of coping with it. Chinese journalists are frustrated to see their investigative piece killed due to political sensitivity, whereas American journalists might grumble about not being able to do investigative reporting at all due to cost cutting. The level of frustration among journalists in these two countries might also be different, with Chinese journalists likely to express more frustration regarding their profession. In other words, aspiration, frustration, and reconciliation (i.e. specific ideals, reality, and compromise for a particular group of journalists) can be examined as key characteristics of a journalism culture.

The aspiration-frustration-reconciliation (or ideal-reality-compromise) framework tackles the unique struggles and experiences of journalists from their own point of view, through probing their ideals, the reality vis-à-vis those ideals, the resulting frustration, and how journalists reconcile the differences between their ideals and the reality. The three aspects are interconnected, as one cannot fully understand the reconciliation without first understanding the aspiration and frustration. Their intricacy forms the basic fabric of the web of meaning for the journalists. The three aspects accommodate the key elements of the occupational culture: thinking and doing, ideas and practices, as well as delicate contingencies regarding the ideas and practices. As such, the aspiration-frustration-reconciliation framework can be useful in exploring the unique occupational culture of a particular group of journalists, all the while stressing a rather holistic view of journalism culture as integrated within specific social and cultural contexts.

Why Metro Newspaper Journalists?

Besides a cultural inquiry of journalism, this book also makes an important contribution to the study of Chinese journalism and journalists, which has come a long way in the past few decades with a growing body of literature. Among the main aspects that have been explored are the regulatory system of the press (e.g., Brady, 2008; Polumbaum, 1994; Schurmann, 1968), investigative journalists (e.g., Bai, 2012; Bandurski & Hala, 2010; Polumbaum, 2008; Repnikova, 2014; Svensson et al., 2014; Tong, 2011), professionalization and professionalism of Chinese journalists (e.g., Burgh, 2003, Li, 1994; Lin, 2010a; Pan & Lu, 2003), Chinese journalists' struggle for freedom of speech (e.g., Hsiao & Yang, 1990; Polumbaum, 1990), and China's press reform in recent decades (e.g., He, 2000, 2003; Liu, 2000; Lynch, 1999; Sun, 2002; Wu, 2000; Zhao, 1998). Together, the existing body of study has researched various aspects of journalism and journalists in China: professional ideology, practice, organization, press system, broader social and political context, as well as actual news coverage.

Why another study on Chinese journalists? While benefiting tremendously from the exciting studies, the current study is different in a couple of ways. The particular group of journalists in the current study is metro newspaper journalists in a second tier metropolis in China. A lot of scholarly attention has been devoted to investigative journalists in China, who are the elite of Chinese journalists, the cream of the crop. Their stories often embody the most intense conflict between the press and political constraints, between journalists and the system, and therefore are very valuable. And yet, there are not many of them and the vast majority of the news workers deserve some attention as well.

Metro paper journalists, in contrast, are the grassroots of Chinese journalists. They are the Average Joe of Chinese journalists, the typical everyday news people. And they have largely been a blind spot in the study of Chinese journalists. A study on this group of journalists fills in this blank and contributes to a more comprehensive understanding of Chinese journalists as a diverse group. Metro newspapers are all market-oriented tabloids, as opposed to Party propaganda organs. They are a new breed of China's press system as a result of a series of reform (see Chapter 2 of this volume for detail). They mainly rely on subscription and advertisement revenue to survive, receiving little to no government subsidy.

Similarly, many studies have focused on journalists in first tier cities like Beijing, Shanghai, and Guangzhou (e.g., Lin, 2010a, 2010b; Polumbaum, 1994, 2008; Zhao, 1998) and relatively few have explored second tier cities in China, which include medium-sized provincial capital cities such as Kunming. It would be misleading to generalize characteristics of journalists in first tier cities as a representative pattern of the whole nation (Lin, 2010b), because China is diverse and not monolithic. By shedding light on a second tier city, my study provides a glimpse into places outside the major metropolitan areas and contributes to a more inclusive understanding of the scene of Chinese journalism.

Why Journalism Culture?

Instead of professionalism, which has been a prominent area of study related to Chinese journalists' ideals and practices, the current study asks a different set of questions: How do journalists give meaning to their work? What does it mean for the journalists themselves to be a member of a particular group of journalists? As valuable as it is, professionalism is more or less nominal, expressing mostly the aspiration part of the entire puzzle. The current study intends to go deeper than "what it should be" and sets out to find other pieces of the puzzle. After the journalists talk about their ideals for journalism, which include professionalism, how do these ideals hold up in reality?

My field study revealed that there is a lot more than trying to be a "professional journalist" in China, because when it comes to actual practice, things don't go exactly as expected. That changes the way the journalists give meaning to their work and changes the meaning of being a journalist in China. In other words, professionalism alone is not adequate in explaining journalism and journalists in China, or other places in the world, for that matter. My goal with the current study is to find a more nuanced approach, well grounded in the field, of explaining, as closely as possible, the whole picture of the world of a particular group of journalists.

The current study deliberately takes a different approach than professionalism also because professionalization tends to compare journalism and journalists in China with their Western counterparts and gauge Chinese journalists against Western norms, and therefore risks missing the true characteristics of Chinese journalists as a distinct group. By asking the question of the meaning of doing journalism, rather than professionalism, the current study was able to seek understanding from the journalists' own point of view and demonstrate, as much as possible, their true color. Rather than professionalization, the current study asks how meaning is given. Rather than from a normative vantage point, the study takes a cultural point of view to accommodate more contingencies and nuances, forming a more comprehensive and intimate understanding of these journalists. The locus of inquiry is not professional norms but occupational culture: a sense of shared meaning and experience; a sense of community.

Structure of the Book

The rest of the book explores this occupational culture through the following chapters.

Chapter 2, The Rise of Metro Newspapers and Metro Papers in Kunming, provides some relevant background information and sets the stage for the inquiry, including China's press reform over the past three decades, the rise of metro papers, the city of Kunming, and some key aspects of Kunming's newspaper industry.

Chapter 3, All the Buzz in the Kunming Newsrooms, draws a sketch of the daily life and work of journalists in newsrooms of Kunming's four metro papers, as a prelude to more detailed analysis of their occupational culture. Aspects touched upon in this chapter include journalists' relationship with tipsters, how journalists are paid, as well as their habitual chain-smoking and lunch rituals in the newsroom.

Chapter 4, Aspirations: Ideals of the Journalists, focuses on the aspirations the metro paper journalists have for their job, including their shared values, ideals, and beliefs. These journalists take seriously their responsibility to the public and aspire to make a difference, uphold social justice, monitor power, and revealing truth.

Chapter 5, Frustrations: Realities of Daily Work, addresses various kinds of restraints journalists encounter—frequent story bans, pressure from the advertisers, and restrictions of the overall media system—and the consequent frustrations.

Chapter 6, Reconciliations: Compromises in Practice, describes different ways through which the journalists reconcile their aspirations and frustrations, such as helping disadvantaged individuals to get a sense of achievement and learning to compromise in their quest of the tougher goal of monitoring the government.

Chapter 7, Journalism Culture in Context: Global Influence, Social Conflict, and Epidemic Mistrust, examines how factors in the broader social environment intertwine with all three aspects of the occupational culture.

Chapter 8, Social Media Impact, takes a closer look at how emerging communication technologies, particularly the use of social media, are changing the game to a certain degree and providing some relief to journalists' frustrations while helping their to achieve their aspirations.

Chapter 9, Journalism Culture With Chinese Characteristics, relates this local journalism culture to broader national contexts, considered in light of previous studies on Chinese journalism, to reveal the Chinese characteristics of the journalism culture. After all, Kunming is part of China and journalists there share many similar views and sentiments with journalists across China. This chapter also proposes a theoretical model of understanding the unique occupational culture of a particular group of journalists through examining their aspirations, frustrations, and reconciliations, as well as the interweaving between these aspects and the broader social surroundings.

Conclusion: Lessons Learned on Studying Journalism Culture, summarizes the traits of the journalism culture found in Kunming and offers final thoughts on how the current study advances related academic inquiry, as well as directions for future research.

Note on Field Research

Before moving to the chapters, I want to note a few things regarding the process of conducting this research. Kunming is the city where I grew up and such a connection helped me gain access to the field. The fieldwork was conducted from July through October in 2011 at all four metro newspapers in Kunming at that time. I spent about 14 weeks doing participant observation and interviews in those newsrooms.

During the first half of my fieldwork, I worked as an editor for one of Paper A's weekly supplements, which featured in-depth coverage on local, national, and international news. At Paper B, I had a gig as a web editor. A little over a month into my field research, I decided to reach out to the other two metro papers in Kunming. I got in touch with an executive of Paper C and Paper D, respectively, through Sina Weibo, China's most popular social network at that time. I gained the permission to observe in the newsroom of Paper C and interviewed the chief editor as well as a veteran from Paper D. I made it very clear from the very beginning, to everyone that I encountered, that I am a scholar from an American institution wanting to do research about journalists in Kunming.

I worked at Paper A and Paper B from mid-July through the end of August, but stopped working from September through late October to focus on research, doing mostly observation with limited participation and interviews. I also accompanied various reporters on nine reporting trips. In addition, I joined several lunch or dinner gatherings with reporters and editors, including an executive's wedding and karaoke party afterwards.

Throughout the field research, I conducted various types of interviews—from the random chat in informal conversation to unstructured interviews without a question list to semi-structured interviews with pre-determined questions to cover (DeWalt & DeWalt, 2001). Most interviews I conducted were one-on-one, semi-structured interviews employing a list of questions I wanted to ask, lasting anywhere between 30 to about 120 minutes. I conducted 49 such semi-structured interviews, although I spoke with more people on other occasions. In selecting reporters and editors to do the semi-structured interview, I tried to choose people of different ages and genders, with various working experiences: young, fresh reporters as well as veteran ones, general assignment as well as beat reporters, and reporters with specialties such as investigative and online reporting. I also interviewed the top executives of the four newspapers.

In general, people treated me very well throughout my fieldwork, except for one incident. I had accompanied a reporter to a hospital pursuing a story about a hospital–patient dispute. We were received by the vice president and spokesman of the hospital, who asked to see our reporter's certificate first thing upon seeing us. The reporter showed him his, and I said I was an intern. The spokesman then said he was not ready to do a formal interview and asked us not to take notes. After a while, as he discussed the incident and voiced his opinions, he seemed to be engaging in a formal interview and I started to take notes. Suddenly the spokesman ordered me:

> "Don't take notes! Give me this page of notes."
> "It won't be in the paper," the reporter said to him very nicely.

But the hospital official insisted on taking my notes. I was a bit stunned by the situation because this had never happened to me in my prior experience as a reporter.

> "We'll give it to you later," the reporter continued diplomatically.
> "Give it to me now! Or I'm not going to do the interview with you," the official said firmly.

The reporter noted good-humoredly that the official was "very stubborn," to which he responded, "I am stubborn."

> "All right. Give it to him," the reporter said to me. So I tore the page from my notebook and handed it over. The hospital spokesman took a look at it, put it down, and said, "Now let's start the interview."
> (September 26, I)

The reporter later said he was sorry that I had to go through the altercation, partly because things like this "won't happen in the United States."

Overall, in the field, I was both an insider and outsider. As far as my origins are concerned, I am an insider, because I was born and raised in Kunming and graduated from a local high school. But in many ways, the city and I have become strangers. I left Kunming at age 19 to attend college in Beijing and have not permanently resided in the city since. Prior to my fieldwork, I've only spent vacations in Kunming, from a few days to a couple of months at a time. During my years away, Kunming, like cities around China, has transformed: old streets and buildings torn down, roads rerouted and highways built, new territories developed, and more. While doing my fieldwork, I found it challenging to navigate through what I once considered my hometown. I got on the wrong bus several times, and often had to call a cab to get to home.

I also had trouble speaking the local dialect, even though I can understand people with no problem, because for 16 years I only spoke it with my family and close friends during phone calls and short visits. For this research, I spoke Mandarin (the national or "common" tongue) when talking with journalists in the field because I was more comfortable using Mandarin as my working language. In fact, Mandarin was often preferable, because many reporters and editors are not from Yunnan, and therefore Mandarin is their working language as well. Those from Yunnan usually speak the local dialect among themselves, but Mandarin is spoken between people from different regions and during group meetings.

I think my connection with the town earned me extra friendliness points, as people were glad to know that I was a Kunming native. At the same time, some seemed wary of my overseas connections and would reconfirm that I was doing scholarly research instead of, say, writing for foreign press, before they would tell me something. Others uttered regrets like "Why did I tell you that?" or "I was not supposed to say that to someone from overseas" after saying something they deemed "sensitive." It is also likely that people withheld certain information altogether. I acknowledge that people's views and perceptions about me inevitably influenced their interaction with me and the information they provided. In order to get the most authentic information possible, I approached people with a modest attitude, listened to them attentively to show my sincerity of learning from them, and always tried to verify information through triangulation (DeWalt & DeWalt, 2001; Lindlof & Taylor, 2002). Whenever possible, I corroborated reporters' accounts about their reporting experiences with published stories, verified facts about the news organizations through written documents and prior literature, and obtained accounts regarding the same event or matter from different sources.

Finally, it should be acknowledged that the current study has its limitations. The scope of the study is limited, focusing on four news organizations in one particular city. The findings are therefore not generalizable, although they can provide some useful insights into studying occupational culture of journalists elsewhere. Due to the tremendous amount of scholarly work that has been done on Chinese journalism and journalists throughout the decades and in recent years, I cannot possibly include all of them into the discussion, despite my best effort to engage as many related studies as possible. The aspiration-frustration-reconciliation framework is also not perfect and can be further revised, polished, or advanced by other scholars or other studies.

Notes

1 This is a pseudo name. Per IRB requirement, no journalists mentioned in this volume is named with their real name.
2 Dates in the parenthesis indicate the date of entry in my fieldnotes. Because all fieldnotes were written in 2011, only month and date will be shown hereafter throughout this volume.
3 Roman numerals at the end of the date indicate the part of the fieldnote for the same date, when the fieldnote is split into more than one part.

References

Bai, H. (2012). 从倡导到中立：当代中国调查记者的职业角色变迁 [From initiative to neutrality: Changes in the professional roles of investigative journalists in contemporary China]. 新闻记者 *[Journalism Review]*, 2.

Bandurski, D., & Hala, M. (Eds.) (2010). *Investigative journalism in China: Eight cases in Chinese watchdog journalism.* Hong Kong: Hong Kong University Press.

Brady, A. (2008). *Marketing dictatorship: Propaganda and thought work in contemporary China.* Lanham, MD: Rowman & Littlefield.

Burgh, H. D. (2003). *The Chinese journalist: Mediating information in the world's most populous country.* London, New York: RoutledgeCurzon.

Carey, J. W. (1992). *Communication as culture: Essays on media and society.* New York: Routledge.

DeWalt, K. M., & DeWalt, B. R. (2001). *Participant observation: A guide for fieldworkers.* Walnut Creek, CA: AltaMira Press.

Geertz, C. (1973). *The interpretation of cultures: Selected essays.* New York: Basic Books.

Glaser, B. G., & Strauss, A. L. (1967). *The discovery of grounded theory: Strategies for qualitative research.* New York: A. de Gruyter.

He, Z. (2000). Chinese communist party press in a tug-of-war: A political-economy analysis of the *Shenzhen Special Zone Daily.* In C. Lee (Ed.), *Power, money, and media: Communication patterns and bureaucratic control in cultural China* (pp. 112–151). Evanston, IL: Northwestern University Press.

He, Z. (2003). How do the Chinese media reduce organizational incongruence? Bureaucratic capitalism in the name of communism. In C. Lee (Ed.), *Chinese media, global contexts* (pp. 196–214). London: Routledge.

Hsiao, C., & Yang, M. (1990). "Don't force us to lie": The case of the *World Economic Herald.* In C. Lee (Ed.), *Voices of China: The interplay of politics and journalism* (pp. 111–121). New York: Guilford Press.

Li, L. (1994). The historical fate of "objective reporting." In C. Lee (Ed.), *China's media, media's China* (pp. 225–238). Boulder, CO: Westview Press.

Lin, F. (2010a). Organizational construction or individual's deed? The literati tradition in the journalistic professionalization in China. *International Journal of Communication, 4*, 175–197.

Lin, F. (2010b). A survey report on Chinese journalists in China. *China Quarterly, 202*, 421–434.

Lindlof, T. R., & Taylor, B. C. (2002). *Qualitative communication research methods.* Thousand Oaks, CA: Sage Publications.

Liu, Y. (2000). 媒体中国 *[Media in China].* Chengdu: Sichuan ren min chu ban she.

Lynch, D. C. (1999). *After the propaganda state: Media, politics, and "thought work" in reformed China.* Stanford, CA: Stanford University Press.

Pan, Z., & Lu, Y. (2003). Localizing professionalism: Discursive practices in China's media reforms. In C. Lee (Ed.), *Chinese media, global contexts* (pp. 215–236). London: Routledge.

Polumbaum, J. (1990). The tribulations of China's journalists after a decade of reform. In C. Lee (Ed.), *Voices of China: The interplay of politics and journalism* (pp. 33–68). New York: Guilford Press.

Polumbaum, J. (1994). Striving for predictability: The bureaucratization of media management in China. In C. Lee (Ed.), *China's media, media's China* (pp. 113–128). Boulder, CO: Westview Press.

Polumbaum, J. (2008). *China ink: The changing face of Chinese journalism.* Lanham, MD: Rowman & Littlefield.

Repnikova, M. (2014). Investigative journalists' coping tactics in a restrictive media environment. In M. Svensson, E. Saether & Z. Zhang (Eds.), *Chinese investigative journalists' dreams: Autonomy, agency and voice* (pp. 113–132). Lanham, MD: Lexington Books.

Schurmann, F. (1968). *Ideology and organization in communist China.* Berkeley: University of California Press.

Sun, Y. (2002). 报业中国 [*Newspaper industry in China*]. Beijing: Zhongguo san xia chu ban she.

Svensson, M., Saether, E., & Zhang, Z. (Eds.) (2014). *Chinese investigative journalists' dreams: Autonomy, agency and voice.* Lanham, MD: Lexington Books.

Tong, J. (2011). *Investigative journalism in China: Journalism, power, and society.* London: Continuum.

Wu, G. (2000). One head, many mouths: Diversifying press structures in freeform China. In C. Lee (Ed.), *Power, money, and media: Communication patterns and bureaucratic control in cultural China* (pp. 45–67). Evanston, IL: Northwestern University Press.

Zelizer, B. (1997/1993). Journalist as interpretive communities. In D. Berkowitz (Ed.), *Social meaning of news* (pp. 401–419). Thousand Oaks, CA: Sage.

Zelizer, B. (2004). *Taking journalism seriously: News and the academy.* Thousand Oaks, CA: Sage.

Zhao, Y. (1998). *Media, market, and democracy in China: Between the party line and the bottom line.* Urbana, IL: University of Illinois Press.

2 The Rise of Metro Newspapers and Metro Papers in Kunming

The so-called metro papers are in contrast to the more conventional Party organs. These two types of media organizations differ in ways of governmental control, style of news coverage, and audience reception. The biggest difference lies in their function: The Party organ serves the Party line (i.e., propagates Party ideas, values, and policies), whereas the metro newspapers take care of the market line (i.e., make profits) (He, 2000; Lin, 2010; Pan & Lu, 2003; Zhao, 1998). In 1999, a meeting of executives from 40-plus metro newspapers around the country agreed upon the following definition of this format: daily newspapers based in a city, market oriented, relevant to readers, and with a strong urban grassroots flavor. In other words, metro papers were "city residents' papers" (Sun, 2002, p. 179).

The Rise of Metro Papers

The metro paper phenomenon was largely driven by the nationwide media reforms in the 1990s, whose main goal was to sever government subsidies to all but a few key Party media organs and thus compel most traditionally government-supported media to become self-supporting. Following the decisive embrace of a market economy at the 12th Party Congress in 1992, many newspapers that for decades had survived on public funds found government subscriptions slashed. A massive movement to market-based financing, with circulation building and advertising becoming critical, ensued (He, 2000, 2003; Lee, 1994, 2000, 2003; Liu, 2000; Sun, 2002; Zhao, 1998). For some small newspapers, this meant the end, but for others, it offered potential for big sales and new life in the marketplace. Major newspaper publishers, mostly those putting out Party organs, scrambled to create new products that would grow their audiences. These state-run news institutions, still receiving some funding from the government to maintain their Party functions but also encouraged to explore other revenue sources, came up with a new breed of popular newspaper that became known as the metro paper (Huang & Zhou, 2003; Liu, 2000; Sun, 2002; Zhao, 1998). By the early 2000s, there were about 500 of them around China (Sun, 2002). The earliest metro papers were created as market-oriented offspring of Party organs. This is the case for *Southern Metropolis Daily*, an offspring of *Southern Daily*, the provincial Party organ of Guangdong; *Spring City Evening News*, offspring of Yunnan provincial Party organ *Yunnan Daily*; and *Western China Metropolis Daily*, offspring of Sichuan provincial Party organ *Sichuan Daily*, among many others. This is because, at the time, Party organs had the financial and human resources to create new publications, and perhaps more importantly, the credentials to obtain licenses for new publications (Liu, 2000; Sun, 2002). Later on, private capital entered into funding some metro papers, such as *New Life Daily* in Kunming. Meanwhile, some government agencies' publications transformed into metro papers, such as *Chengdu Business News* (Huang & Zhou, 2003).

These metro papers may be categorized as "semi-official" commercialized newspapers, and in some cases as "non-official" fully commercial newspapers (Stockmann, 2010). Official papers continue to publish as explicit mouthpieces of Party apparatus and government agencies, financed by a mix of some type of state subsidies and advertising. Fully commercialized papers are financed solely through advertising, retail, and investment and run as profit-seeking enterprises. In between are semi-official papers, still affiliated with Party or government organs but oriented toward and sustained by the market. Commercial and semi-official papers are less controlled by the state and have more variety and flexibility than official papers.

Metro dailies often arose in the major regional metropolises, usually provincial capitals, populous cities that function as economic, cultural, and political centers. As such, these cities are the key market for selling advertisements (Liu, 2000), with circulation fueled by attention to local news—metro papers are generally local papers (Huang & Zhou, 2003; Sun, 2002). And in contrast with the common parent papers—municipal or provincial organs printed on broadsheets—metro papers are almost invariably in tabloid format and employ much livelier language, headlines, layout, and graphics. Unlike official papers, which emphasize government or Party news and maintain a serious tone, metro papers traffic in stories of common people as well as celebrities, entertainment, and sensationalism. Some metro papers also are bold about criticizing those in power (Liu, 2000; Sun, 2002; Wang, 2008). These traits have made metro papers an enormous success in many cases, read by millions every day on the bus and subway, at work, or at home, influential enough to gain a strong hold in the mainstream discourse (Huang & Zhou, 2003).

Last but not least, metro papers compete fiercely with each other. One-paper towns are nearly nonexistent in China, especially in provincial capital cities. In Guangzhou, at least three local daily papers are competing for circulation and advertising: *Guangzhou Daily*, *Goat City Evening News*, and *Southern Metropolis Daily*. In Chengdu, capital city of Sichuan, there was a time when five metro papers were vying for preeminence. In Nanjing, capital city of Jiangsu, at least three metro papers are major players. And in Kunming, the capital city of Yunnan and research site of the current study, there used to be at least six metro papers, and four remained at the time of my fieldwork, fighting for market share in a city of six million people (Huang & Zhou, 2003; Liu, 2000; Sun, 2002).

Metro papers operating in the same city, targeting similar readership and competing for the same stories and advertisers often turn out, not surprisingly, quite similar in appearance and content. Their competitive battles entail reducing prices, adding pages, increasing color, and rewarding subscribers— to name just a few tactics (Huang & Zhou, 2003; Sun, 2002). The metro papers in Kunming are a case in point.

Metro Papers in Kunming

Kunming is about 2,000 miles southwest of Beijing. It is the capital city of Yunnan Province, a multiethnic province bordering Myanmar, Vietnam, and Laos and very close to Thailand and Cambodia, which are all members of the Association of South East Asian Nations (ASEAN). Kunming has become China's land gateway to ASEAN member nations, and is forging strong economic and cultural ties with these countries. The city is also a major tourism destination that attracts visitors from all around the world. At the end of 2010, there were 6.4 million residents in the city (Kunming Bureau of Statistics, 2011).

Yunnan is the province in China with the most variety of minority ethnic groups: 25 such groups out of the total 55 formally recognized are represented in Yunnan. Historically, Yunnan has always been regarded as a borderland occupied by non-Han, and therefore outside the mainstream Han culture. The very name of Kunming was originally that of an ethnic group residing in the eastern part of the region before it came to refer to the place. Yunnan is up to this date considered a remote, border province and somewhat exotic place, comparing with eastern China regions, where the core of traditional Chinese culture was nurtured. It is also perceived as among the less-developed provinces, in terms of economy, society, and culture. Nonetheless, Kunming has one of the most dynamic newspaper industries in the country, of which the city's four metro papers are an essential part.

Spring City Evening News (hereafter *Evening News*), a market-oriented tabloid published by the provincial Party organ, *Yunnan Daily*, was founded in 1980 and is said to be China's first evening newspaper created anew in the post–Cultural Revolution era. Such reader-appealing evening newspapers were the harbinger of the later metro papers. It soon gained popularity for criticizing government work and officials' corruption, as well as celebrating the multiethnic culture of Yunnan (Wang, 2008). In the late 1990s and early 2000s, as part of the trend of publishing market-oriented metro papers, a few other metro papers were created, including *City Times*, first published in 1999 by the municipal Party organ, *Kunming Daily*; *Dianchi Morning News*, another metro paper by *Yunnan Daily*; and *East Continent Times*, first published by Yunnan Propaganda Department; plus *New Life Daily* (hereafter *New Life*) and *Yunnan Information Daily* (hereafter *Information Daily*) (Wang, 2008).

New Life is the reinvention of a publication of Yunnan Association of the Handicapped, a semi-official organization under the direction of the provincial government. People from the association sought investments from a private company based in Fujian, which still ran the advertisement department of the paper at the time of this study, and transformed the paper from an agency publication into a market-oriented metro paper in 2000 (Jia, 2010). First published in 1985, *Information Daily* used to be the publication of Yunnan Planning Committee, a government agency. Its metro-paper makeover was carried out by *Chengdu Business News*, a successful metro paper based in Sichuan, Yunnan's neighbor province, which invested in the paper and reinvented it in 1999 in an attempt to claim a share of the Kunming market (Xu et al., 2009). In the past few years, some of the papers failed to survive the market competition. At the time of this study, there were four in the market: *Evening News*, *City Times*, *New Life*, and *Information Daily*.

Among them, *Evening News* and *City Times* are the offspring of the provincial and municipal Party organ, respectively, and could be regarded as semi-official papers. *New Life* received investment from a private enterprise. *Information Daily* was then a joint venture of Guangzhou-based Southern Daily Group and Yunnan Publishing Group, both state-owned enterprises, with Southern Daily Group controlling editorial matters. These two papers could be seen as commercialized papers (Stockmann, 2010). All four papers are metro papers, as opposed to the party organs in Kunming, namely, the *Yunnan Daily* and *Kunming Daily*. The current study was conducted at the four metro papers.

Like same-town papers elsewhere, metro papers in Kunming engaged in fierce competition. Kunming is seen as one of the top 10 most competitive media markets in China (Xu et al., 2009). The first metro paper founded in Kunming was the *Evening News*. From 1980, when it was first published, through 1999, the *Evening News*' popularity and market dominance was unchallenged, until *Chengdu Business News* invested 6 million yuan in *Information Daily* and taught a lesson to the Kunming news industry on how to run a metro paper. Not long after *Information Daily* was launched, so was *City Times* (Xu et al., 2009). The newspaper war in Kunming was well underway.

Information Daily was a quick success in terms of profits, and it encouraged other government agency publications to follow suit, among them was *New Life* (Xu et al., 2009). Other new comers around that time included *East Continent Times* and *Dianchi Morning News*. The newspaper market in Kunming was all of sudden full of smoke. In 2000, to gain an edge in the competition, *City Times* started a price war, selling at just 20 cents RMB per copy (about 3 cents USD). Other metro papers scrambled to reduce their retail prices, which eventually caused huge losses to the papers. At one point, the retail price became so low that some retailers sold new copies of the newspapers to paper recycling facilities instead of readers to make a bit more money. To keep things under control, Yunnan propaganda authorities set a minimum price at 50 cents RMB per copy (Xu et al., 2009).

But the newspapers later came up with new gimmicks to reduce the price. In early April 2006, *New Life* introduced an innovative method of subscribing: renting the paper. Readers pay only a fraction (36 yuan, about US$6) of regular annual subscription, provided that they save all the old copies for *New Life* staff to come collect at the end of the year. *New Life* would then sell these old copies as recycled papers and get some money back. In early June, the *Evening News* responded by reducing its annual subscription to 60 yuan (about US$10). In mid-June, *City Times* reduced its fee to 30 yuan. Two days later, the *Evening News* further reduced the price to 25 yuan, something unheard of in China up to that point. The next day, *City Times* reduced its subscription to a new low of 20 yuan per year. *Information Daily* followed suit, setting its one-year subscription at 20 yuan (Chen, 2006; Xu et al., 2009).

Besides the price war, Kunming metro papers also fought a circulation war, each claiming to have higher circulation than their competitors did. One day in June 2000, *City Times* announced that Kunming Credential Office verified the paper's daily circulation to be more than 104,000. The next day, the *Evening News*, widely regarded as the number one metro paper in Kunming, claimed that it had a daily circulation of no less than 150,000. Meanwhile, in an article published in the *Evening News*, newly created or transformed metro papers were denounced as aiming for high-profit, low-price dumping and publishing exaggerated or fabricated stories, which was more or less the case (Xu et al., 2009). *New Life* soon joined the argument and released the number of copies ordered to be printed every day, ranging from 130,000 to 200,000, as a proof of its daily circulation (Xu et al., 2009).

Harsh competition, especially the brutal price wars, brought wounds to all metro papers and forced them to consider other ways to compete. They came to realize that a better, more rational way to compete was to enhance the quality of news and establish their own specialty and personality (Chen, 2006; Sun, 2002; Xu et al., 2009). From 2006 onward, all four remaining metro papers have been readjusting their positions, constantly going through page makeovers, changing their mottos, and redefining their personality. The *Evening News*, which claims the top spot among the four in terms of influence, fame, and income, focused on news on Kunming as well as on other cities and regions in Yunnan. The *City Times* put a lot of emphasis on local news. In 2003, *Chengdu Business News* withdrew its funding from *Information Daily* due to disagreement with other publishers of the paper. In 2007, *Information Daily* received investment from Southern Daily Group, the parent group of *Southern Daily* and *Southern Metropolis Daily*, and took a new life. The paper set its sight on and beyond Yunnan, and showed strong interests in covering ASEAN countries. As for *New Life*, it claimed to be focusing on providing news that was of high value, namely, original, in-depth reporting and investigative journalism (Xu et al., 2009).

Such competition, chaos, and even losses among Kunming's metro papers were also experienced by other local markets across China, to various degrees. Like elsewhere in China, Kunming metro papers learned and grew through these battles and contests. Journalists and executives of these papers learned to do better journalism as well as better marketing, readers learned to discern good papers from bad ones, and the media market grew and matured. In a region that has traditionally been viewed as economically and culturally backward, Kunming's newspaper industry actually has gained a lot of national attention through its dramatic competition, and the industry itself is seen as at an upper-middle level in the country (Chen, 2006; Sun, 2002; Xu et al., 2009).

New Players: The Internet and Social Media

Since China officially connected with the global Internet in 1994 (Peng, 2005), the Internet and related technologies have played an increasingly important role in journalism practice in China. Nearly every media outlet in China, newspapers and broadcast stations included, national and local media alike, now has a website (Peng, 2005); and news has become a major component of commercial web portals such as sina.com and sohu.com, although such commercial websites are not allowed to cover political news by themselves and may only republish content from state-sanctioned news organizations (Lagerkvist, 2006; Peng, 2005).

The Internet has certainly contributed to breaking through the state monopoly on information, with more diverse opinions than ever available online, leading some observers to speak of an online public sphere in China (Tai, 2006; Zheng, 2007). Such online public discourse gained further momentum with the introduction of weibo,[1] or microblogging, services.

Adopting Twitter's standard, each post on weibo cannot exceed 140 Chinese characters, which actually accounts for considerably more content than the same number of English alphabet letters—140 Chinese characters is equivalent to roughly 70 words. Chinese microblog sites first emerged in 2007 on a relatively small scale. What turned weibo into a national sensation was the launch of Sina Weibo in 2009, a service provided by China's most influential web service and content provider, sina.com.cn (Yu et al., 2011).

Within two years, Sina Weibo gained 300 million registered users. By 2011, there were on average 100 million posts on Sina Weibo each day (Zhou, 2012). Research has shown that 78% percent of Sina Weibo users are under 30 years old, and 66% percent are college educated. Journalists fit well with this profile. Moreover, more than 25% of Sina Weibo posts are about news and social issues (Yu et al., 2011). As with Twitter, the system allows common folks to obtain and share news and information among themselves rather than going through gatekeepers of traditional media. Weibo is no longer few-to-many, but everybody-to-everybody communication, and this service is playing an increasingly important role in the development of China's civil society.

Not surprisingly, Weibo (i.e., Sina Weibo) has become an indispensable part of Chinese journalists' daily work. This is evident from Weibo's involvement in spreading information about public events over the past several years. In September 2010, for example, a family in Jiangxi set themselves on fire to protest government-ordered demolition of their home. When two sisters of the family tried to go to Beijing to plead their case to higher authorities, local government officials sent people to capture them at the airport. The sisters eventually had to hide in a restroom to avoid being captured and called a reporter for help. The reporter posted the situation on Weibo, and the post was retweeted more than 2,700 times in one morning. Consequently, the incident was followed by many media as well as the public, who voiced strong support for the victims and eventually prompted the government at a higher level to investigate the case and punish responsible local officials (Lee, 2011).

As will be discussed in a later chapter, Weibo is playing an increasingly important role in Kunming journalists' practice.

Note

1 Throughout this volume, lower case "weibo" refers to microblogging in general; capitalized "Weibo" refers to Sina Weibo, the most popular weibo service in China, which Chinese journalists mostly use.

References

Chen, P. (2006). 乱战——昆明都市报业价格 "肉搏" 警示录 [*Price war among metro papers in Kunming*]. Retrieved March 13, 2012, from http://news.xinhua net.com/focus/2006–07/27/content_4865345.htm

He, Z. (2000). Chinese communist party press in a tug-of-war: A political-economy analysis of the *Shenzhen Special Zone Daily*. In C. Lee (Ed.), *Power, money, and media: Communication patterns and bureaucratic control in cultural China* (pp. 112–151). Evanston, IL: Northwestern University Press.

He, Z. (2003). How do the Chinese media reduce organizational incongruence? Bureaucratic capitalism in the name of communism. In C. Lee (Ed.), *Chinese media, global contexts* (pp. 196–214). London: Routledge.

Huang, S. M., & Zhou, Y. (2003). *A new century of China media markets*. Beijing: CITIC Publishing House.

Jia, M. (2010). 一份报纸的创新十年 [Ten innovative years of a newspaper]. In M. Jia (Ed.), 我们:生活新报十年志 [*Us! The ten years of new life daily*] (pp. 1–5). Kunming, Yunnan: Yunnan People's Publishing House.

Kunming Bureau of Statistics. (2009). *Statistic report on economy and social development in Kunming in 2008*. Retrieved April 5, 2011, from http://www.km.gov.cn/structure/xwpdlm/tjxxxx_100459_1.htm

Lagerkvist, J. (2006). In the crossfire of demands: Chinese news portals between propaganda and the public. In J. Damm & S. Thomas (Eds.), *Chinese cyberspaces: Technological changes and political effects* (pp. 59–77). London: Routledge.

Lee, C. (1994). *China's media, media's China*. Boulder, CO: Westview Press.

Lee, C. (2000). *Power, money, and media: Communication patterns and bureaucratic control in cultural China*. Evanston, IL: Northwestern University Press.

Lee, C. (2003). *Chinese media, global contexts*. London, New York: Routledge.

Lee, K. (2011). 微博改变一切 [*Micro-blog: Changing the world*]. Shanghai: Shanghai University of Finance and Economics Press.

Lin, F. (2010). Organizational construction or individual's deed? The literati tradition in the journalistic professionalization in Chinese. *International Journal of Communication, 4*, 175–197.

Liu, Y. (2000). 媒体中国 [*Media in China*]. Chengdu: Sichuan ren min chu ban she.

Pan, Z., & Lu, Y. (2003). Localizing professionalism: Discursive practices in China's media reforms. In C. Lee (Ed.), *Chinese media, global contexts* (pp. 215–236). London: Routledge.

Peng, L. (2005). 中国网络的第一个十年 [*The first decade of China's online media*]. Beijing: Tsinghua University Press.

Stockmann, D. (2010). Who believes propaganda? Media effects during the anti-Japanese protests in Beijing. *The China Quarterly, 202*, 269–289. doi: 10.1017/S0305741010000238

Sun, Y. (2002). 报业中国 [*Newspaper industry in China*]. Beijing: Zhongguo san xia chu ban she.

Tai, Z. (2006). *The Internet in China: Cyberspace and civil society*. London: Routledge.

Wang, Z. (2008). 云南新闻史话 [*History of Yunnan press*]. Kunming, Yunnan: Yunnan University Press.

Xu, J., Zhou, Z., & Wang, Z. (2009). 昆明报战十年志 *[Ten-year newspaper war in Kunming]*. Retrieved March 13, 2012, from http://media.people.com.cn/GB/10060129.html

Yu, G., Ou, Y., Zhang, B., & Wang, B. (2011). 微博，一种新传播形态的考察 [*Weibo—Examining a new form of communication*]. Beijing: People's Daily Press.

Zhao, Y. (1998). *Media, market, and democracy in China: Between the party line and the bottom line*. Urbana, IL: University of Illinois Press.

Zheng, Y. (2007). *Technological empowerment: The Internet, state, and society in China*. Stanford, CA: Stanford University Press.

Zhou, W. (2012). 新浪微博注册用户突破 3 亿 微博商业化进度有望加快 *[Sina Weibo registered users surpass 300 million]*. Retrieved March 14, 2012, from http://finance.21cn.com/newsdoc/zx/2012/02/28/10968459.shtml

3   All the Buzz in the Kunming Newsrooms

Like many newsrooms around the world, the ones at Kunming's local papers operate long hours. At the metro papers, a typical day starts at around 9 a.m., when reporters are required to report to the newsroom—or have notified their editors as to their whereabouts. Normally, the newsroom is rather quiet before noon, with no more than half the reporters sitting at their computers, some trying to figure out what story to work on. The place becomes abuzz in the afternoon, when people return from reporting to write stories and editors start their shifts.

Most editors come to work at 3 p.m. and usually do not get off until past midnight. Working until 3 a.m. the next morning is commonplace. Editors will have a budget meeting close to 5 p.m. to share their current story lists. Night is their busiest time, when they have just a few hours to edit stories, decide on graphics, and put the final pages together. Everything is processed electronically: Reporters submit stories through an intranet, and editors fetch stories from the computer database, edit them, and send them over to designers. By the time the last light is turned off in the newsroom, it often is just a couple of hours before the lights will be turned on again for the new day.

Tipsters, BBS, and eBikes

Reporters at Kunming's metro papers often rely on calls to a telephone "hotline" and leads from the Internet to find news stories. A group of "news tipsters" in Kunming traverses the city every day trying to find stories in the streets and typically calling all four metro papers with the same tips. If a tip results in a published story, the tipster will receive about 50 yuan (about US$8), and some people manage to make a living this way. The metro papers rely heavily on this channel, which seldom delivers exclusives: all four papers end up running some of the same stories on most days.

A reporter from Paper C, for instance, has formed a rather solid working relationship with at least one tipster over the years. Once when I was accompanying this reporter outside his newspaper, his regular tipster phoned about a car collision right in front of the newspaper building, and the scene was still there when we got back to the building. The tipster was there, too, and the reporter introduced him to me. I asked the tipster why the crashed cars were still blocking the way, and he said the police had come, but could not move the vehicles (September 23, I)—it seemed like he was doing some reporting as well.

Besides these usual callers, it seems few other people call into news hotlines. Reporters and their editors say hotline calls have declined dramatically in recent years, partly because people are getting used to posting news tips on online bulletin boards or via social media. Consequently, reporters' daily routine also includes searching through popular BBS sites and Weibo postings for news stories.

Upon receiving an assignment, reporters need to figure out how to get to the site of news. Taxi, public transportation, company vehicles—reporters use whatever is the most convenient and available. Many reporters own the sort of battery-powered bicycles, or eBikes (electronic bike), which are ubiquitous in Kunming. They look very much like motorcycles but do not burn gas, and are lightweight, flexible, faster, and more powerful than a person-powered bicycle, and certainly much more affordable than a car.

I took one rather nerve-wrecking ride with a photographer on the back of his eBike. We dodged heavy traffic, sometimes against the traffic flow, and had what seemed to me numerous close calls with other eBikes, conventional bicycles, and motor vehicles. I finally screamed when our eBike nearly hit a bicycle running down a hill at a high speed. Just when it seemed to me that none of the bikes would stop in time to avoid the collision, they both stopped abruptly. No one was wearing a helmet (August 19).

General Assignment vs. Beat Reporters

Reporters in the newsroom generally fall into two groups: those on general assignment, called "hotline reporters" or "societal reporters," and those covering regular beats. Hotline reporters responding to phone tips typically cover car accidents, construction site accidents, migrant worker protests, and sometimes individual altercations—stories out in the streets involving common folks. Beat reporters, on the other hand, mostly cover stories related to government agencies and officials.

Being a hotline reporter is where most new reporters start honing basic reporting and writing skills. Gradually, some hotline reporters develop strong connections with sources in certain areas and become beat reporters, covering government, law enforcement, education, health, or other areas. Their leads now come mostly from news releases, official websites, or notification from spokespersons, and they often attend government meetings and news conferences. The logistics of work may be easier, but now they face the challenge of extracting relevant stories from the bureaucracy and obtaining information from officials who may be hard to reach or reluctant to speak to the press.

General assignment reporters sometimes encounter adventure, but the work is hard and the challenges not always pleasant, such as when a heavy-duty truck transporting soil and sand from construction sites ran over an electronic bike, which happens quite often in a booming city. A young reporter was sent to one of such accidents one day and posted a photo on his Weibo showing a dead body lying in the street, followed a few minutes later by his message of discomfort: "I want to throw up now. Any suggestions, anybody?" About 40 minutes later, he posted more photos, including a closer view of the dead body, and warned, "One of them is bloody, and it is advised that people with a small stomach not look. I have vomited many times upon seeing it, anyway." Another 20 minutes later, he posted again: "I am going downstairs to buy a beer. Hopefully it will relieve my discomfort."

Getting Paid

Although working tough and challenging jobs, reporters' income is rather moderate. They get monthly paychecks, with the amount on the paychecks determined by both quantity and quality of stories they contribute, although different newspapers use different schemes to calculate pay.

At Paper A, for instance, editors assigned a numeral score to each story their subordinate reporters wrote in the past month based on the size and the quality of the story. Typical scores may be 200, 500, or 1,000, corresponding to the amount of money, in yuan, that a story is deemed to be worth. That is to say, a story with a score of 500 would be paid 500 yuan. By the time I finished my fieldwork, Paper A was modifying its evaluation and payment policies. Paper B used a different, more sophisticated system. Editors assigned each story a letter grade (A, B, C, D), with a formula that incorporates factors such as exclusive or in-depth story to convert the letters to a numerical value, which together with another measure on the size of the story produced the amount of money the story was worth. Both newspapers required reporters to turn out work amounting to at least 1,500 yuan per month—the minimum performance requirement. Failing to meet this requirement results in a warning and, if bad performance persists, firing.

On one payday at Paper A, an editor commented to an underperforming reporter who was getting about 1,000 yuan for the month: "Is that enough for travel expenses for you and your girlfriend?" It was close to the National

Day holiday, when everybody would get a whole week off. Another reporter got 4,000 yuan, which was fairly good (September 27).

Reporters' incomes may vary drastically from month to month, ranging from less than 2,000 yuan to more than 8,000 yuan, whereas that of the editors and executives is more stable, usually around 5,000 yuan. Higher ranked executives make more. Staff also receive benefits, such as health insurance and housing subsidies, although the details vary from newspaper to newspaper and from individual to individual. Generally speaking, however, compensation for news workers in Kunming is lower than that for other white-collar workers. To make some extra cash, moonlighting is not uncommon among journalists. For example, some reporters write longer versions of stories they covered and sell them to magazines not affiliated with their own news organization.

In comparison, journalists in Guangzhou, a first-tier mega city in southern China, were making more money. A study shows that roughly 59.7% of surveyed journalists had monthly incomes between 5,001 and 10,000 yuan. Unlike most journalists in Kunming, Guangzhou journalists' incomes have two components: fixed salary and monthly bonus, with the latter determined by some kind of evaluation system, based on the quantity and quality of their work. For many journalists, bonuses comprise a bigger portion of their monthly income than fixed salaries (Lin, 2010).

A shadier, but openly acknowledged, source of additional income for reporters is the so-called red envelope commonly handed to those covering press conferences, product promotions, business openings, and other publicity occasions. Each red envelope usually holds a few hundred yuan in cash, the assumption being that favorable stories will result. In the past, red envelopes have been viewed as a form of rampant corruption among Chinese journalists (Zha, 1995). But in Kunming during my fieldwork, the issue rarely came up. One veteran journalist mentioned to me that beat reporters sometimes get red envelopes (October 21, II), and an executive told me he did not care whether reporters receive red envelopes or not, as long as they produce good, relevant stories (October 18, II). On the other hand, reporters are not allowed to take outright bribes from sources—defined as larger amounts of cash given secretly in exchange for cover-up or favorable coverage.

It needs to be noted, however, that the red envelope issue not surfacing that much during my fieldwork should not be taken as an indication that the practice has become obsolete. It might well be that journalists in my study were not willing to tell a researcher from the U.S. too much about this kind of unethical practice or they had taken it for granted and did not bother to mention it.

Cigarettes, Air, and Food

It is hard to find a male staff worker who does NOT smoke right in the newsroom. Men smoke everywhere: at their desks, during meetings, while writing stories. It is easy to tell which computers belong to men: the ones with keyboards covered with ashes. There is no such thing as a cigarette break, because people who wish to smoke may do it anytime, anywhere. Whenever two or more men are in the same room, one or another will hand out cigarettes to male colleagues—an expected ritual of greeting and showing respect. In one newsroom where I worked, I happened to have a chain-smoker sitting in the adjoining cubicle. He smoked incessantly for hours, which from day one I found quite horrid. I did not protest because smoking in the newsroom is commonplace (July 20).

I finally asked a group of heavy-smoking editors why they did not care about their health, and they said they had gotten used to smoking. One editor said if China had banned smoking in public, he would not smoke so much. Right away, another argued that if China ever banned smoking in public, Yunnan's economy would collapse—Yunnan has China's biggest tobacco company with an annual profit over 30 billion yuan (about US$4.6 billion). Another joked that their smoking contributed a lot to the GDP of Yunnan (August 22).

At another paper, an editor said that some reporters developed smoking habits to deal with deadline pressure, and recalled his own experience of that: "After a day's reporting, all I wanted to do most was to sleep. But I couldn't. I still had to write the article. But after a few cigarettes, I felt better" (July 28). In short, among the men of the newsroom, there seems to be a sense of collective denial: They all know smoking is unhealthy, but it is a vice they wholeheartedly share.

On the other hand, I did not see a single woman smoke in the newsrooms I visited. Instead, a lot of women have a humidifier on the desk, and the streams of mist from these small portable devices mingle with the tobacco smoke floating in the newsroom air (July 25). Women told me they used humidifiers simply for humidifying, because they found the newsroom too dry and stuffy (July 28). Both newsrooms I worked in occupy a huge warehouse-style space covering an entire floor of a building. Cubicles and dividers demarcate different sections and individual desks, and windows are invariably closed. No wonder the women are starved for better air, even as the men seem mindless of the smoke-laden oppression.

Cigarette or humidifier, both men and women need to have lunch. The most common way of having lunch is phoning for take-outs and having the food delivered to the desk. They sometimes chip in to order food to share, like a mini feast. One day, a reporter and I came back to the newsroom just in time to join a group of reporters and editors lunching around a round table. They ordered a big pot of *gan guo ji*, steamed and stir-fried chicken with chili peppers, lotus roots, mushrooms, peanuts and other stuff, plus a big bowl of vegetable soup—splitting the cost of about 100 yuan total. They had plenty and invited us to sit down, so we squeezed in at the already crowded table, tore an empty foam box into two as our plates, and found some chopsticks from a reporter's desk drawer.

While eating, people chatted randomly. They started to gossip about who had a crush on whom in the newsroom. An editor, a man, started to tell about an ex-girlfriend, while another editor, a woman, gave running commentary like a talk show host. Everyone else was rapt with attention as they finished the food. I helped clean up—having been told it was a rule that whoever finished last clears the table (October 10).

Under other circumstances, dining out becomes an after-work social gathering. One evening, I joined about 20 something journalists from one paper for a feast that featured lots of liquor, lots of cigarettes, and some dirty jokes. The actual eating seemed secondary. A photographer passed his iPhone around the table to show caricatures of his colleagues he had made using an app, producing much laughter, as well as a mini-contest to identify the people in the pictures. The conversations were a mix of jocular and serious, including some actual work discussion. Everybody clearly was having a great time (July 19).

References

Lin, F. (2010). A survey report on Chinese journalists in China. *China Quarterly, 202*, 421–434.

Zha, J. (1995). *China pop: How soap operas, tabloids, and bestsellers are transforming a culture*. New York: New Press.

4   Aspirations
Ideals of the Journalists

As already stated in Chapter 1 of this volume, this study essentially tries to answer the question of how journalists give meaning to their work, and therefore it is a study of journalism culture, or the occupational culture of a particular group of journalists. If culture is the system of meaning that guides human actions and allows them to make sense of their day-to-day behavior, then the occupational culture of journalists is the system of meaning that guides journalists' professional action and allows them to make sense of what they do as journalists. An occupational culture contains two major dimensions: networks of meanings contained in sets of shared, sometimes taken-for-granted beliefs and values, or the *substance* of the culture, and mechanisms for expressing and affirming these beliefs, or cultural *forms*, including practices, behavior, myths, ceremonies, symbols, languages and gestures, and rituals and rites (Schudson, 1997/1989; Trice, 1993; Trice & Beyer, 1984). The specifics of the substance and form of an occupational culture are formed uniquely in the context of a particular occupation (Guzman et al., 2008).

These notions of occupational culture miss one piece of the puzzle: What if the substance and form are not always in sync? In other words, the sets of shared, taken-for-granted beliefs and values sometimes only describe what journalists aspire to be, not what they really have become. In fact, during my field research, a striking finding is precisely the mismatch between journalists' practices and what they aspire to do. Instead, there is a gap, a discrepancy, between what they think (and say) they should do and what they actually can accomplish. It is therefore necessary to seek another conceptual framework that fits and works better for the specific situation under investigation, with a grounded theory approach (Glaser & Strauss, 1967).

Through sorting through and analyzing data gathered from the field, I came up with three new categories—aspiration, frustration, and reconciliation—and integrated them into a new theoretical framework. In this theoretical framework, journalists' professional aspirations (i.e., shared values and ideals of what they think journalism should achieve) is only part of the occupational culture, as these aspirations do not always materialize. Depending on the specific social and professional circumstance, journalists, as a group, face different kind of obstructions that impede them to fully achieve their aspirations, resulting in different levels of frustration. Therefore, the actual meaning the journalists give to their work, the palpable ways through which journalists render their work meaningful, is often a compromise between their aspirations and the reality. I call such a compromise reconciliation. A more comprehensive understanding of a particular journalism culture, especially an understanding that captures the uniqueness of a particular group of journalists under specific social, cultural, and professional circumstances, calls for examination of these journalists' professional aspirations, frustrations, and reconciliations.

This chapter addresses the aspirations of metro paper journalists in Kunming: what they regard as the ideals and values of being a journalist.

Monitoring Power

In talking about the kind of journalism they aspire to do, journalists often mention the notion of "monitoring" or *jiandu*, which is akin to the watchdog notion. During the reform period, the idea that news media should monitor public power was raised by journalism scholars in the 1980s, and the Party, in part, has welcomed the concept but also imbued it with qualifications. Propaganda officials allow that the mass media have the function of monitoring the behavior of officials and the performance of the Party and government, but at the same time, they set various boundaries. These may include requiring prepublication review of coverage of sensitive topics or even of mentions of names of officials. Also, the monitoring function tends to be more acceptable at the provincial levels and above, whereas the local press and especially commercial tabloids are more restricted in this regard (Wei, 2006).

An investigative reporter who has taken the idea of monitoring power to heart his entire career said that, "Journalism should be the conscience of the society" (October 14). Another veteran journalist said the value of the media's very existence rests on monitoring public power as the only way to "push the society forward" (September 27, I). An executive said journalists who "want to save the society through news coverage," even if it involves revealing the ugly side, incorporate the most passionate and pure ideals for journalism (October 18, II).

Some of my informants expressed admiration for investigative journalists, saying the nickname of "darkness-revealing journalists" (*jiehei jizhe*) captures the enterprise well. "Darkness-revealing journalists, monitoring journalists, they are the real journalists," said an editor who used to do

investigative reporting himself. China lacks sufficient numbers of such journalists, he said, for obvious reasons: The job entails threat and risk without
necessarily bringing high income, especially in this piece-rate era, because
a single story can take a very long time to report. "That is why in China it
is so hard to be a journalist who has the real sense of justice, someone who
reveals the darkness, monitors power, and really wants to push for social
progress" (September 27, I), he said. In Kunming, hard-core investigative
journalists are clearly viewed as being in a league of their own—a minority
of icons to be praised but not necessarily emulated.

Upholding Social Justice

Most of my informants expressed strong desires to help people in need,
something they take as part of their mission not simply out of sympathy.
In a society experiencing widening gaps between social strata, journalists
see helping the disadvantaged as a matter of promoting social justice. One
young journalist called helping the disadvantaged a matter of conscience.
"Under China's system, many unfair things happen. What media people
should do is to uncover these things," she said (September 20). Another
reporter said media should help the disadvantaged "because strata at the
bottom of the society have no basic rights" (October 8, II).

Some informants maintained that if journalists don't help these people,
nobody would. "Journalism is a label. Without this label, I cannot help any-
one. I still want to use my profession to help more people," said a reporter
(October 25). "They are already powerless. If newspapers don't speak for
them, nobody will speak for them," said an editor. He also acknowledged
that, for market-oriented newspapers, being on the side of common folks
can help to sell papers, because those are the readers (August 30).

Chinese journalists don't have to look far to find problems facing the urban
poor, migrant workers, and others who encounter hardships and often violations of their rights. It's not unusual for ordinary people to actively seek help
from the press, often by simply walking into a newsroom and telling someone about their problems. Increasingly, people who feel wronged will stage
some kind of protest—typically referred to as *nao*, or a "disturbance"—to
attract reporters, because chances are news tipsters will see the action and
call it in. As for why disadvantaged people so eagerly seek help from journalists and why journalists are receptive, many of my informants agreed the
fault lies with China's political system, under which people without money
or power have little recourse.

"In China's system, the channels of reporting to the government are not
very open," noted an investigative reporter. "If a matter is not publicized,
the government would push it aside as much as possible" (September 26, II).

Another reporter said avenues for common people to convey requests to authorities are neither smooth nor wide. "When they have no other way to go, the media provide them with a channel that can go around the bureaucracy" (September 23, II).

Others pointed out that legal approaches for common folks to defend their rights often do not work in China, with many laws being empty words that cannot be enforced. "If the law often exists in name only, common people can only resort to the media, because the media have a little bit special power," said an editor. "They can publicize situations where the law is not enforced. Once [things are] publicized, there will be some public pressure and such pressure definitely can push for solving problems, defending people's rights and seeking justice" (September 27, I).

As a result, "for disadvantaged groups, the easiest institution to go to is the media," said a veteran journalist. "Government agencies are very cold to them. When talk to the media, they can release their emotions and feel better" (October 8, I). An editor put it this way: "Why do people come to the media? Because they have no other place to go. Coming to the media has the lowest cost: They won't be beaten up, nor locked up. When they come, there will be a cup of tea and someone listening. For some people, just to let it out is good" (October 11, I).

Journalists hope, and so do those who turn to them for help, that making problems known to the general public through publication of news stories will prompt government attention and resolution. Indeed, this sometimes is what happens. But journalists also say that if media coverage helps to solve one person's problem, hundreds more will follow suit. "Somebody blocks the road once [to protest something], the media covers it, and government agencies solve the problem," said a veteran journalist. "Then . . . too many people try to jump from buildings or block the road—the people have gotten the bad lessons from the media" (September 22, II). Journalists say they are gradually getting tired of these kind of incidents, but still need to cover them, and more or less still sympathize with people's desperation.

Journalists understand, of course, that any influence they have comes from the publicity of their media platform, and that publicity can only do so much. They know they lack any authority to actually dictate anybody's business. An editor who is a strong proponent for social justice and representing the disadvantaged acknowledged that media "can never have direct effects, because the media have no executive power." In his view, "The media can only monitor some darkness and evil through revealing the truth, which puts pressure on the ones being monitored. Of course, even with such pressure, attention from the leaders is still needed. Leaders have to say something and give some instructions . . . That's the situation in China" (September 27, I).

Making a Difference

One commonly expressed desire is to make a difference through news coverage. A web editor who used to be a reporter, for example, said journalists all want to see some results from their work. "If [we] don't think this way, there is no meaning to being a journalist," he said (September 16). An editor who was a reporter for many years expressed hope that news stories can make a difference and redress injustice. "I hope my own relatives, my parents won't be treated unfairly when something [bad] happens," he said (September 21).

Among the changes journalists say they desire to prompt are fairness, justice, social and economic development, freedom and democracy, and the search for truth (October 19, I; October 11, II). One reporter spoke of working toward a society in which people from different social strata can all find ways to make a living and will receive fair treatment and rewards, saying this hope compels him to "condemn unfair occurrences" (September 16). An executive who is also a veteran reporter listed "democratization of politics, marketization of the economy, and diversification of culture" as "the standards of a good society, good country." He added that the roots of evils in China's society always trace back to the political system, saying, "If the political system is the most important factor, then does it not mean that we should change it?" (September 18).

All three objectives stated above are associated with the idea of revealing truth. "Truth is in short supply in China," said the same executive. "Seeing truth can even be very [emotionally] moving" (September 18). For him and many other journalists, revealing truth is the foremost and ultimate job for journalists.

These findings more or less echo with earlier studies on Chinese journalists' professional outlook. Several studies have demonstrated that journalists find occupational meaning in the opportunity to monitor authorities, serve common people, and promote social justice (Burgh, 2003; Chen et al., 1998; Polumbaum, 2008).

One of the studies maps out Chinese journalists' professional aspirations as including four ideal-type professional orientations along two dimensions: level of commitment to journalistic independence and to advocacy (Hassid, 2011). Journalistic independence refers to the idea that news workers themselves should determine standards of newsworthiness, regardless of the preferences of the authorities. Advocacy refers to journalists' willingness to stand up for causes they believe in, even when these causes might be politically risky. These four types go beyond a more conventional dichotomy of Western professionalism vs. Party journalism to include two more types: advocate journalists who have a strong desire for social change and workaday journalists, who care for little but money or steady employment. Workaday journalists are present in my study as well, and they tend to be the ones who complain about too much work for too little pay and express plans to seek other jobs. For example, a young female reporter said she originally was thrilled about becoming a journalist. "I thought journalists were awesome! On TV, I saw reporters seeking justice for common people, unstoppable everywhere, super sharp!" Now, after a year, she was thinking about quitting. "Being a journalist is hard work, and the compensation is very poor," she said. "The money I make in one month is only enough for me to buy one piece of clothing!" (September 21).

There are many better, easier ways to make a living than being a journalist in China. For those who have chosen to be and stay being a journalist, there is always something beyond just to make a living. No matter if they lean toward independence or advocacy (Hassid, 2011), a lot of the journalists I know, through my working experience in China and the fieldwork, are really committed to one thing: making China a better nation. That, above all, is their ultimate aspiration. It is not to say that they are fanatical patriots. They are simply citizens who care about the future of their country and their fellow citizens.

Like many previous studies, these four types in Hassid's study (2011) mostly address the ideals, or aspirations, of the journalists: what they think they want to, or should be. But what happens when their ideals run into the wall of reality? Knowing the aspirations is only part of the inquiry. When it is evident through field research that these aspirations do not necessarily turn into actual action and journalists express tremendous frustration, more probing is needed.

References

Burgh, H. D. (2003). *The Chinese journalist: Mediating information in the world's most populous country.* London, New York: RoutledgeCurzon.

Chen, C., Zhu, J., & Wu, W. (1998). The Chinese journalist. In D. Weaver (Ed.), *The global journalist: News people around the world* (pp. 9–30). Cresskill, NJ: Hampton Press, Inc.

Glaser, B. G., & Strauss, A. L. (1967). *The discovery of grounded theory: Strategies for qualitative research.* New York: A. de Gruyter.

Guzman, I. R., Stam, K. R., & Stanton, J. M. (2008). The occupational culture of IS/IT personnel within organizations. *The Data Base for Advances in Information Systems, 39*(1), 33–50.

Hassid, J. (2011). Four models of the fourth estate: A typology of contemporary Chinese journalists. *China Quarterly, 208,* 813–832.

Polumbaum, J. (2008). *China ink: The changing face of Chinese journalism.* Lanham, MD: Rowman & Littlefield.

Schudson, M. (1997/1989). The sociology of news production. In D. Berkowitz (Ed.), *Social meaning of news* (pp. 7–22). Thousand Oaks, CA: Sage.

Trice, H. (1993). *Occupational subcultures in the workplace*. Ithaca, NY: ILR Press.

Trice, H. M., & Beyer, J. M. (1984). Studying organizational cultures through rites and ceremonials. *Academy of Management Review, 9*(4), 653.

Wei, Y. (2006). 新闻传播法教程 [*Media and communication law*] (2nd ed.). Beijing: People's University Press.

5   Frustrations

Realities of Daily Work

Simply based on their aspirations, one might say these Chinese journalists are rather powerful in their capacities. But the aspirations often are only aspirations, not the reality. As put by one reporter, media are viewed as an "all-capable institution," but actually, "the media are not power agencies, and journalists are rather powerless" (September 27, II). In fact, my fieldwork revealed that the journalists' desired meanings of work often are not fulfilled in practice. Why so? The answer, I would suggest, lies largely in the myriad constraints, obstacles, and limitations that the journalists in Kunming face in their daily work. The many constraints significantly shape this journalism culture, and journalists' responses to the constraints—cognitively, symbolically, emotionally, and in practice—also constitute an essential part of their occupational culture. This chapter discusses these constraints and journalists' responses.

Obstructions to and Troubles From Reporting

Upon setting out to cover stories, journalists often can expect to face obstructions to their reporting. A reporter told me about an experience several years earlier when he and two colleagues arrived at a local court in a small town for a hearing. After they had been sitting in the courtroom for a short while, the judge suddenly adjourned the hearing. Next thing they knew, a few court police officers had surrounded them and were asking what they were doing there. The officers also attempted to grab the reporter's audio recorder by force and in the process scratched his neck, events caught on camera by the photojournalist in the group. "Whoa, that was too big. [The officers] insisted on smashing the camera. Now it was even harder for us to get away," the reporter recounted. The three of them were then detained separately in three rooms and questioned by court officials trying to figure out the purpose of their visit, because the case was rather sensitive. The officials also took away their keys, cellphones, and recorders. Eventually, the officials asked the journalists to sign off on the interrogation record. They refused. The officials would not let them go. Finally, my informant said, he signed, putting the date and a comment that the court had "made three reporters from the provincial capital encounter the darkest day in journalism history." They were finally released (September 27, I).

Interference with reporting does not always come from government. A photojournalist of 10 years related a nasty scare he and some colleagues had while covering a coal mine accident. The coal mine had released a death toll of three, but some tipsters reported a death toll of 11. The discrepancy was important because three deaths would only require reporting to the provincial authorities, whereas 11 deaths required reporting to the central authorities. "The boss of the mine threw a bag of money in front of us, and told us, 'If you guys do not take this bag of money, I will use it to buy your lives.' I deleted materials in my camera right in front of him." After leaving the mine, they filed the story and fled the town in a hurry, without even checking out at their hotel (October 16).

In addition to obstructions to the reporting, journalists may face retaliation afterwards. One investigative journalist I interviewed is even writing a book about such experiences. On his computer, he showed me his draft manuscript, which includes 20 cases. Going down the table of contents with his cursor, he enumerated the first three: "This one almost cost my job, this one almost cost my job, and this one almost cost my life." In the aftermath of his reporting on problems at a mine in a small town, for example, the township government tried to smear him in an online posting. The allegation was that the "dark heart reporter" had taken a bribe of more than 10,000 yuan. Consequently, the reporter was investigated by provincial authorities, and was finally cleared of a charge that would have destroyed his reputation. "After this incident, I kept silence for a while," refraining from investigative assignments, he recalled. "Later my name was cleared, but there is always a shadow." He's now more reticent in taking on investigations, he said, "I think it over, whether or not it is feasible." He also thinks about his family. "After having a kid, I feel the society is too complicated, too dangerous. I no longer have the same passion as before" (October 12, II).

Along with obstruction or retribution against individual journalists, news organizations may face trouble after running stories reflecting badly on powerful interests. This can range from verbal complaints to official warnings, directives to write self-criticisms, and even lawsuits. "There are high risks for doing in-depth, watchdog coverage," said an experienced editor. Authorities and subjects of such stories would come back with attacks on the paper, he said, adding that he himself had penned many of the required self-criticisms. While I was doing my fieldwork, Paper A was in the midst of trying to fend off a libel suit the plaintiff had filed in response to a story documenting how he and his thuggish brothers bullied their fellow villagers.

Story Bans

To some journalists, danger, threats, and difficulties are simply challenges to be surmounted. Some journalists even find being detained by local authorities rather thrilling. What journalists cannot stand, however, is when their stories are killed even after they have gone through all that bother and considerable risk.

The journalist who was detained and then released by a local court had such an experience. After being let go, he recalled, "The three of us were extremely excited. We realized that the biggest story had just happened!" That night, with no access to a computer, he and his colleagues wrote about the incident by hand in great excitement. With the help of a local post office staffer, who also had a lot of complaints about the local court, they managed to fax the story back to Kunming around 2 a.m. At that point, the editor in charge hesitated, and told the reporter that consultation with provincial judiciary authorities had determined that this incident would paint a negative image of Yunnan's judiciary system, and therefore the story would not be published. "I argued with him on the phone, and slammed down the phone," the reporter said. "I continued to argue with him after returning [to Kunming], slapped the table in front of him, and went on strike for a while." But nothing could bring the story back to life (September 27, I).

Jin ling, or story bans, are all too familiar to journalists in Kunming. They may get issued before reporting has begun, but often they arrive when reporting is well underway or completed, or, as with the example above, when the story is written and ready for the presses. Indeed, the prospect of story bans figures into newsroom routines.

An experienced and especially enthusiastic investigative reporter who has a great deal of familiarity with story bans told me about going to a mountainous area in northern Yunnan to investigate alleged illegal mining. She finished the story and it was killed, because Tibetan people inhabited the area, which made any reporting from there politically sensitive. "I was pretty upset," she said. "I now can accept the fact that some stories won't be published, but I still try to finish them." The story was eventually filed as an "internal reference," or *neican*, reports that officials above a certain rank can read but are not accessible to the public. The reporter said she knows internal references are read by decision makers, but she prefers letting the readers know first, and then having the government solve the problems. "Only this way, [media] can push for social progress and let people take warnings," she said. "Internal references can only solve individual cases, but have no warning effect for the entire society" (September 26, II).

Besides straightforward bans to avoid particular stories, or bans that kill stories before they get to the press, newsrooms receive all kinds of coverage guidelines from propaganda authorities. The day after a high-speed train collision in Wenzhou in July 2011, which generated a media frenzy on both social and traditional media, the following directives regarding coverage of the collision arrived at a Kunming newsroom: 1) Rely mainly on the [national] Xinhua News Agency release, 2) demonstrate governmental and social rescue efforts, and 3) do not speculate or make associations. These guidelines were received by an executive, who passed the message to his editors (July 24). The third item reflected authorities' concern that people would link the accident to broader social problems, such as the aggressive pursuit of economic growth at the price of public safety and possible corruption behind the failure of the track signaling system, apparently the direct cause of the accident. This is a typical case where potential political ramifications prompted efforts to quash media coverage in the hopes of containing public anger.

Political sensitivities are not restricted to domestic news. In another example, an editor was planning a multipage overview of the U.S. Occupy Wall Street movement. He had collected all the articles he wished to use when, a day before everything was to be laid out, he received a text message of a propaganda directive saying Occupy news should be downplayed. Specifically, it banned any extensive coverage, including attention to public rallies, and also called for restraint on journalists' own microblog postings. The package-in-progress was killed. "Sometimes the propaganda authorities are nonsensical," the editor said. "I can only obey the rules of the game: do it when allowed, stop when prohibited, no need to argue, and no need to think about whether it is reasonable" (October 21, II).

The Red Line

Kunming journalists all know to be wary about the "red line" (*hong xian*), or the absolute boundary beyond which they cannot go. But nobody can delineate the line absolutely. One reporter enumerates antigovernment comments and stories that could shake social stability or undermine unity among ethnic groups as off-limits (September 6). An executive says red line topics for metro papers include religion, ethnic minorities, military, and the political system. "China is not like the U.S., which has a constitution to protect freedom of speech," he said (October 12, I). In fact, Article 35 of the Chinese constitution *does* promise citizens the right to "freedom of speech, of the press, of assembly, of association, of procession and of demonstration," but unlike with the U.S. First Amendment, nothing in China's law prevents Party and government powers from trumping those rights.

At one editorial meeting, a chief editor warned his staff of the risk of using Weibo as a source for stories, saying, "If you use one wrong item, it could bring fatal consequences to the paper." He then stressed the importance of having a good grasp of the red line. "These days doing media work is like walking on a tightrope or by the cliff. If you have no guts, the market and public will reject you. If you dare too much, the Party and government will reject you" (July 25). At another meeting, the same chief editor cautioned against too much emphasis on issues such as protecting basic human rights, but still urged his staff to go beyond pure news and dare to demonstrate some values and "attitudes" (*taidu*) as long as they did not step over the red line. "We are trying to survive in the cracks," he said (September 13).

Indeed, for metro papers, business success hinges on being audacious and outspoken without stepping over the red line. This is partly to fulfill journalistic ideals of acting as watchdog and speaking for the people, and partly to gain an edge in the harsh competition among local papers. As one executive put it: "Without monitoring [power], [the newspaper] will have no attraction. This is the law of the market" (October 12, I). At the same time, the double requirement of being bold and hewing to the proper side of the red line inevitably poses a dilemma, and figuring out the balance is a challenge journalists face every day.

Business Pressure

Political pressures have long been salient to Chinese journalists, but increasingly, requests and complaints from advertisers have created new tensions for newsrooms. A Kunming chief editor was stunned to learn in an editor's meeting that China Mobile, the country's biggest mobile service provider, could fine his newspaper for publishing a story naming the company if the company did not like the story. Some editors said the paper had paid a 100,000 yuan deposit to China Mobile when the company purchased advertising, under an agreement that if the paper ran stories harmful to China Mobile, fines would be deducted from the deposit. The chief editor immediately called in the executive in charge of ads and asked why he had signed such an agreement. It turned out that this was standard practice and the chief editor could do nothing, except to tell his staff that in the future, any negative items involving China Mobile should avoid mentioning the company's name (August 31).

A reporter at a different paper encountered something similar when he went to cover a fire at an office building, where he ran into a staffer from his paper's advertising department. She had gone there to deliver some gifts to a client, the very company that occupied the burning building. Back in the newsroom the woman from the ad department found the reporter and asked him if he could leave the company's name out of his story. The reporter replied that, "If the name is withheld, the location will not be clear, and the truthfulness [of the story] will be undermined. This needs to be decided by the higher leaders." The woman left and came back with the directive, "Withhold the name." She said an executive had made the decision, and added, "Sorry for troubling you. Just use the name of the building, not its [the company's] name, and it will be fine. I don't want to do things like this either." The reporter replied, "Don't worry about it" (September 1).

The ad head at one paper said companies often worry about being named in news stories out of concern for "unexpected effects" and fear of giving readers "misunderstanding of the brand," even when all the facts are correct. He attributed this to consumers' mistrust toward businesses in China nowadays. "Consumers' suspicions are influenced by the broader environment in China. Businesses lack credibility, and consumers do not trust them," this executive said (October 13).

King Without Crown vs. Migrant Worker of News

Given all these obstructions, most journalists interviewed for this study rejected the idealized notion of journalists as "kings without crowns"—a widely used label for journalists in China that implies a sense of nobility along with the ability to accomplish the impossible, and a saying one executive called "pretty much empty talk." He added, though, "But the tool of media is very important. Journalists hold this tool in their hands and have the right to speak. It is also not exaggerating to say journalists are the fourth estate, in terms of how they create trouble for the government." At the same time, he maintained, "Journalist actually is just a regular occupation, like lawyers and doctors, serving the society through providing useful information. They shouldn't think too highly of themselves" (October 12, I).

One young reporter described journalists as a disadvantaged group with no legal protection. Even if they have the right to cover news, she said, "Who offers you the right to cover news? There is no legal boundaries either. To say that journalists are kings without crowns is probably talking about the Republic of China era. It is not the case now" (October 21, I).

Instead, journalists interviewed for this project commonly used another label for themselves: "migrant workers of words" (*wenzi mingong*) or "migrant workers of news" (*xinwen mingong*), which is similar to "news labourers" mentioned in another study (Svensson et al., 2014, p. 7). In China, the term contract worker (*da gong de*)—used in contrast with permanent worker—highlights the difference between working outside versus within the establishment. Contract workers are hired on temporary basis, with contracts, usually renewable, lasting one to five or more years, and may be fired at any time. Their benefits are not government subsidized and their salary is based mainly on piecework—in the case of reporters, on the amount and quality of articles, photographs, or other items they finish that see publication. Permanent workers, on the other hand, are employees of the state-run system, typically with government-subsidized health benefits, pension plans, and housing, and sometimes lifetime tenure. Other studies have also noticed these two types of employment of journalists in other Chinese cities: market-based contract system (*he tong gong*), wherein journalists' jobs are based on a contract, and the bureaucratic quota system (*shiye bianzhi*), wherein journalists are treated as members of the government staff. The journalists in the quota system seem to be more stable than those in the market-based contract system are (Lin, 2008).

Up to the reform period, all media employees (indeed, most nonagricultural workers generally) were in the quota system. The contract system began to emerge in journalism about 20 years ago, producing the coexistence of secure and contract forms of employment in news organizations. There is a clear-cut distinction between the two statuses. A perhaps apocryphal story has it that one year, when a Party newspaper in Kunming distributed bonuses of salted fish to its staff for the Chinese Lunar New Year, within-system workers got a whole fish, whereas outside-system ones received only a half (October 21, II).

Such a difference between the within and without is largely a result of China's transition from a centrally planned economy to a market economy. The permanent worker is a legacy of China's socialist era, when all urban employees, including media workers, were considered as hired by the government and entitled to all kinds of benefits provided by the state, from salary, health care, childcare, schooling, and retirement to even funeral services. The market reforms in all sectors have changed human resource policies, and permanent hiring—what used to be called the "iron rice bowl" *or tie fan wan* when salaries were uniformly low—is being phased out across industries and replaced by a contract arrangement. Among news media, the market-oriented metro papers mostly depend on contract workers.

At Kunming's metro papers, this includes the top executives. The very few permanent news workers are mostly with Party organs, and their numbers are diminishing as older workers retire and permanent positions diminish. A study found that in Party organ newspapers in Guangzhou, 65% of respondents were in the quota system and 35% were in the market system, whereas in market-oriented newspapers, 22% were in the quota system and 78% were in the market system (Lin, 2010). The vast majority of journalists at the metro papers in Kunming, all of which are market-oriented, are contract workers. Throughout my fieldwork, in fact, I only encountered one permanent worker, who joined a Party-affiliated metro paper as a reporter more than 10 years earlier. As far as I know, he is also the only one among the journalists I talked to who has a monthly base salary not related to the actual amount of work he accomplishes and lives in an apartment provided by his news organization. Contract journalists have to purchase commercial housing on their own.

Thus, journalists likening themselves to migrant workers of words/news arises from their job status: They are hired on a temporary basis with no guarantee of long-term employment, no security, and no certainty about their livelihoods—perhaps not as tenuous a situation as that of migrant workers who leave their rural villages to seek job in cities, but shaky nonetheless.

The analogy also reflects journalists' sense of their social status: Many feel they are despised by the establishment, similar to migrant workers being scorned by the rich and powerful—for reasons that are both similar and different. Government and Party authorities tend to view contract employees as somehow less legitimate than permanent employees are, and that extends to journalists. One news executive said this makes interviewing people from government agencies, who tend to be permanent civil servants, all the harder because "they look down upon journalists, knowing you are hired by contract." He added that civil servants consider *Yunnan Daily*, which is the provincial Party organ, the mainstream paper, whereas metro papers like his are nonestablishment and thus of lower standing (September 22, II).

A third reason for journalists to draw the analogy with migrant workers is their relatively low incomes that most consider far less than their hard work really deserves—as with migrant workers, who often do the toughest physical labor for little reward. Journalists are not shy about this complaint. At one editorial meeting, an editor told his editor-in-chief that the newspaper's housing subsidy of 100 yuan (about US$15) per month to help people afford housing was too low, and lower than that of other local news organizations. "You cannot even buy one square meter after saving for several years. What's the point?" he said (August 17).

An executive at another paper, who told me, "I consider myself a migrant worker of words," openly worried about his income. "I often think, what should I do when I am old? The housing subsidy every month is 120 yuan, and the mortgage for my house is 2,600 yuan per month. A friend of mine has a housing subsidy of 1,200 yuan per month." And he bemoaned how he thinks society looks upon his occupation. "Journalists look like kings without crowns, appearing to be shiny, but actually have very low social status. Isn't there a saying? Watch out for fire, burglars, and reporters!" (September 14, September 21). Indeed, this is a well-known phrase that journalists often use as a self-mocking joke.

Frustrated, Disappointed, and Conflicted

Obstructions to reporting, retaliation after reporting, story bans, limitations imposed by political and commercial forces, and perceived low social status all contribute to cultivating a profound sense of frustration and disappointment among journalists in Kunming, injecting conflicted meanings into their occupational culture.

A photojournalist reflected on his decade-long experience as a journalist, "Coal mine owners trying to buy your life, thugs beating you up, riot policemen surrounding and kicking you, all these things just for a few bucks of remuneration, and sometimes your stories don't even get published. Would you still have the will to do the job?" He said he "absolutely" had ideals at the beginning of his career, but now found his heartfelt journalistic ideals getting "smashed by reality." He blames the larger society. "This nation has no faith. Right now the biggest faith for people is money. China right now is a world for the rich and powerful. A handicapped man who stole an electronic bike to send his wife to see a doctor was sentenced to seven years in prison. A son of a rich family who murdered someone got two years of probation outside prison" (October 16).

Indeed, some reporters find it hard to be enthusiastic under these circumstances. One young reporter says that as a result of "too many" story bans, "I have become numb. Now I don't even bother to touch sensitive topics. Even if I did the story, I would be doing it in vain." She related how a group of reporters once spent a month investigating an environmental pollution story, only to see it shelved. "We were very upset at that time. We even said if the story was not allowed to be published, we'd resign together and go establish an independent investigative group. Now that I think about it, we were really very naïve back then. So passion dies little by little" (September 27, II).

For many reporters, frustration emerges or continues even after stories are printed when no real change seems to follow their revelations of problems or wrongdoings. "Can you tell the truth? Is there any use to tell the truth? Any value in the story?" said one editor. "If after publishing the story, there is no impact whatsoever, what is the value of the story? What is the value for the media to exist? I am rather pessimistic." He added, however, that to some degree media can function as a watchdog and push for social progress—just not as much nor as fast as he would hope (October 26).

It then comes as little surprise, therefore, that journalists with a strong desire to make a difference also express a strong sense of frustration over how little difference they can actually make. A veteran journalist put it in this way in an essay he wrote about his career:

> Being a journalist has its pains and joys . . . when we help others through news coverage, we can be ecstatic. Faced with many social

realities that we cannot remedy, we really want to cry out. Because being a journalist is just an occupation, we are not almighty. We want to help everyone who needs help, but that's impossible. We wanted to reveal all the discords in society, but that's impossible.

What a journalist can do, he told me, is to "learn the background of an issue" and try to prompt the authorities to investigate. "Otherwise there will be no effect after publishing the story" (September 22, II).

A young reporter who professes to have been inspired by Oriana Fallaci to become a journalist and dreamed of becoming a war correspondent described how her experience has eroded her ideals:

> I definitely hope to change something. I fantasize that I report on a corrupt official, and the official will be sacked; report on unreasonable policies, and the policies will be overturned. But in reality, I found out that journalists are powerless. One corrupt official is sacked, and the next one may be more corrupt. A policy is already in place, and it is not something a journalist can shake.
>
> (September 27, II)

She went on:

> My dream is being broken little by little . . . I now doubt the value of journalism. I used to think journalists could realize their own dreams, say what they want to say and do things others cannot do. I used to think being a journalist was valuable and meaningful, not just for wages. Now I feel that actually being a journalist is just a job.
>
> (September 27, II)

Then she clarified, "My pessimism for journalism is not toward the profession itself, but toward the general [social] environment in China" (September 27, II).

This kind of disappointment, not just toward news work per se, but toward the government, the entire society and system, even the country, is rather prevalent among Kunming journalists. An investigative journalist who cares deeply about environmental issues is disappointed about insufficient environmental protection. She said,

> [The government] should protect the environment for the future generation, but officials only want political accomplishments, attracting investments and business, occupying farmland to build industrial parks. Many are energy-consuming, heavily polluting projects that are

destroying the environment. I am hurt and worried watching all this, but I cannot solve the problem. There is nothing I can do.

(September 26, II)

She wiped tears off her face while saying this to me.

"They talk about the Chinese dream," one editor said in the middle of the newsroom. "My dream is to leave China. After all these years, I'm very disappointed with this country" (August 30). He later told me that covering societal news for many years had shown him too much of the dark side of society.

At the beginning, I loved my country very much. Later I saw too much, and came to feel this country has too much injustice and makes common people's lives miserable. So if there is an opportunity, I will go live abroad. Maybe I am too extreme. I am often very sad, and can't help but thinking, what if my parents encounter these [bad] situations, what can I do?

(September 21)

With often passionate aspirations and high expectations on the one hand and deep frustrations and often bitter disappointment on the other, Kunming journalists speak of feeling *jiu jie*, or entangled, struggling, wrestling, contradicting, conflicted, an overarching term they use quite often.

A young reporter said the obvious gap between his dreams and reality is what makes him conflicted. He became a journalist because he wanted to "pursuit the journalistic ideal that cannot be realized," he said.

China's system has too many problems, and I aspire to a free and democratic society. . . . but this ideal is basically impossible to realize. Everybody has such an ideal at the beginning. Overtime, the reality wears away the ideal. So [we are] very conflicted.

(October 11, II)

"Journalists indeed are conflicted. There is pain every day," said a veteran journalist. "I also have turned from an idealist to a pessimist. There is progress, but not enough. I also dream that media controls will be lifted someday, but my dream is ruptured time and time again" (October 21, II).

An executive summarized the conflicted feeling among journalists as follows:

It is torturous to be a journalist in China. You first face a huge rupture—the conflict between story bans and your desire to report the truth.

Basically these story bans are intractable. You just can't do anything. Second is capitulation to commercial interests, especially among metro papers. Third, this is an occupation that cannot guarantee high income . . . many Chinese journalists now cannot afford housing, the very basics for living. This makes people feel deeply frustrated. In addition, as a reporter you also feel frustration over the [poor] effect of media coverage.

(September 18)

But is there any way they can still render their job meaningful for themselves? The next chapter answers this question.

References

Lin, F. (2008). *Turning gray: Transition of political communication in China 1978–2008*. Dissertation. University of Chicago, Chicago. Department of Sociology.

Lin, F. (2010). A survey report on Chinese journalists in China. *China Quarterly*, *202*, 421–434.

Svensson, M., Saether, E., & Zhang, Z. (Eds.) (2014). *Chinese investigative journalists' dreams: Autonomy, agency and voice*. Lanham, MD: Lexington Books.

6 Reconciliations

Compromises in Practice

As already demonstrated, journalists in the current study face all kinds of constraints: risks during covering news, troubles after publishing critical stories, story bans, and no or little real impact. These journalists want to make a difference, and yet have their hands tied by political and economic interests. They have the desire to make the country a better place, but time after time, they see corruption, unfairness, and injustice being repeated, even getting worse, and cannot help but doubt the virtue of the entire system, even losing faith in the country. Consequently, most journalists in this study expressed confliction, frustration, and disappointment to various degrees. In practice, many journalists found ways to compromise and reconcile their ideals with the not-so-ideal reality, as discussed in this chapter.

Helping People While Doing Journalism

Many journalists invest great energy and even get personally involved in helping others while doing news work, and they have plenty of tales to tell. An editor recalled an incident six years earlier, in which a man walked into the newsroom to say he wanted to post an advertisement looking for someone—the birth parents of his daughter, whom he had picked up from a cardboard box left on the roadside 10 years before. The man said that over the years, he had rescued 21 abandoned babies, most girls, and later found them homes either with their birth parents or with adopted parents, except for this one girl whose birth parents were nowhere to be found, even though he knew their names from a note left with the baby. The man was poor, making a living by collecting and recycling trash and waste, and he did not want the girl to live like that forever.

Moved by the man's kindness, the editor, then a reporter, not only wrote four rather long stories but also became actively involved in searching for the girl's parents. They were able to find the girl's aunt, who told the girl that her parents had abandoned her because they wanted a boy. Already having a girl, they did not want to pay the fine for violating the one-child policy for a girl. They later did have a boy. Ultimately, the girl gave up trying and decided to stay with the man who had brought her home. By this time, the stories had become national news. The baby rescuer was interviewed by several other media outlets, including CCTV, China's authoritative national network, and the reporter also was interviewed by national TV and choked up a dozen times while telling the story as he thought about the man and child "living in the middle of piles of trash, keeping each other company in a crammed 10-square-meter room." The reporter's sympathy, emotional investment, and active involvement in the story brought the case national recognition along with moral, financial, and material help for the man and the girl. "I felt that as a journalist, I can indeed help people," the reporter (now an editor) said (September 22, II).

In some cases, reporters willingly take on the role of agent for the powerless in dealing with authorities, such as this reporter who met with a teenage girl who had come to the newsroom seeking help. The girl, whose parents were migrant workers in Kunming, could not participate in high school entrance exams because she did not have registered residence in Kunming, which meant she had no chance to attend high school in the city where her parents were working. Even though the girl and her parents had brought their case to the court and gained a favorable verdict, the ruling cannot be enforced because the local education authorities would not cooperate.

The reporter visited the family's cramped home and accompanied the girl to the Yunnan Education Administration offices. "Now government agencies wouldn't give a damn about a common folk," he said. "If she went alone, nobody would even look at her. If she came with a reporter, they would pay attention, because if it showed up in a newspaper, the leaders would criticize them. They are afraid of that." (August 9). After several attempts to talk to the educational officials, the best response they got was that the girl could take the exam the next year (October 8, II).

As a matter of fact, not only are individual journalists willing to help people from lower social strata, their news organizations are also participating in similar projects, which is called *gong yi*, or philanthropy. News organizations' enthusiasm for philanthropy has become a new trend in China. Such projects are initiatives to protect or help satisfy grassroots constituencies, from providing assistance to the poor or undertaking environmental protection to helping sick migrant workers. Several high-profile journalists have come out in support of such a philanthropic approach, including Deng Fei, a senior editor at the *Phoenix Weekly*, who promotes free lunch programs for schools in less-developed areas (Guo, 2011). A newspaper executive interviewed for this study hails the journalists-turned-social activists behind such undertakings as pioneers, and he says frustrated journalists can find greater satisfaction by working with philanthropic initiatives that produce real results. The executive's paper actively supported Deng Fei's school lunch program, saying combined efforts have pushed China's education ministry to take the idea seriously enough to start an official trial for future expansion of the program. "He [Deng Fei] pushed the government to carry out a big philanthropic project, and this is very satisfying," the executive said. "Suppose I just ran a story about some students cannot afford lunch at school, can it make much impact?" (September 18).

Sense of Achievement

Journalists in this study are nearly unanimous in saying their incomes fail to match the efforts they expend in their jobs, and yet most still find their work worthwhile. Despite dissatisfaction over pay and status, despite the fact that many speak of arduous-but-fruitless endeavors, quite a few of my informants pointed to the possibility of "helping others" as the main reason they think their hard work is worth it. In response to the question about which of their stories gave them the strongest sense of achievement, most journalists I interviewed gave examples related to helping those in need. Among 21 accounts of such stories in my fieldnotes, 14 concern helping those in need (the rest are stories related to scoops, revealing truth, and having some social or political impact). Among them are a migrant worker who slept in a sewer tunnel (September 26, I), a young woman who had jumped from the fourth floor of a building to escape a rapist, injuring her spine and fracturing her pelvis (September 22, I), and an 8-year-old girl who rescued her 1-year-old brother from a house fire and suffered severe burns (September 6). These were all people with low income and little means. In each of these cases, the news story generated thousands of dollars in readers' donations that helped the migrant worker to go back to his hometown and the other two to get much needed medical treatment. "Because I can help others, do something for others, I feel the value of my existence," said the reporter who wrote about the young woman (September 22, I).

Another reporter interviewed some veteran soldiers from the Republic of China era, who had been conscripted by the Kuomintang government during World War II to fight the Japanese in the remote locales in Yunnan, even crossing the border to fight in Myanmar. Mostly forgotten since the Communists took power, some of these veterans lived in disparate parts of Yunnan's mountainous areas, lonely and deprived. The reporter recalled visiting one of them on a rainy, foggy night, riding in a vehicle traveling along slippery, curvy, and steep mountain roads: "That was the most difficult and most horrifying road I have ever traveled," she said. "The steering wheel of the vehicle kept turning on its own, out of control. It took us 2 hours to drive

7 kilometers (about 4 miles). I thought I was going to die on the road." Once at the soldier's home, she found, "there was nothing, just a few wooden stools. Coal ashes were everywhere. His bed was nothing but some hay and worn-out cotton wadding on the floor." The reporter felt proud that her story made more people pay attention to these abandoned veterans, but even more important was the actual personal visits. "For these veterans, making them feel that there is finally someone paying attention and acknowledging them is the biggest comfort of their lives. Some veterans cried the moment they saw you" (September 27, II). To her, such emotional comfort is the biggest help she provided to these forgotten heroes.

Learning to Compromise

Despite all sorts of obstruction and difficulties, journalists in these metro papers managed to do some watchdog journalism, albeit not as often and strong-handed as they had wished. In this process, what they really have learned to master is to compromise between their aspiration and the reality.

Watchdog coverage often casts authorities in an unfavorable light, and journalists must navigate their relationships with authority figures with care, because the agents of government and other centers of power control much of the information the newspapers rely upon. Journalists in Kunming frequently meet up with government officials over meals and alcohol for the purpose of what they call *gou tong*, or communicating.

The first time I met an executive at Paper C, he was on his way to have lunch with some government officials. "They need to communicate with me about city patrol beating up a street vendor," he told me. City patrol, commonly known as *cheng guan* in China, is a local law enforcement force in charge of maintaining the order of the city, including busting street vendors who have no government permission to conduct business. Many times such confrontations turn violent, and the executive's paper apparently had run stories about such an incident. The officials weren't necessarily going to give him trouble, he said. "They just want to communicate. They are not very happy. It's a *Hongmen yan*" (September 7). "Hongmen yan" is an ancient Chinese legend involving a dinner scheme to murder invited guests, and the executive used this term to indicate the hostile nature of the meeting.

It's not unusual for journalists and news executives to be invited to such meetings after publication of critical stories on government agencies and officials, on businesses, or on rich and powerful individuals. The host inevitably will request the newspaper to stop pursuing certain coverage, or even to run favorable stories to counter any negative impact. Sometimes, the journalists would comply to avoid souring the relation with the government, losing advertising accounts, or facing a lawsuit.

These journalists see the need to carefully handle what they call "both open rivalry and veiled strife" relation between journalists and authorities. One cops and courts editor said he had to pick his fight, and he would push for in-depth investigation only on certain issues. He said authorities in the past might openly boycott a paper that ran unfavorable stories, announcing that they would not accept interview requests from that paper. But the "hard boycott" is practiced less and less, in part because a paper can disclose what is happening on the Internet, prompting public criticism. The authorities have wised up and now the fear is a "soft boycott" (*ruan fengsha*). The editor said that without announcing any boycott intention, the authorities simply do not inform a paper about news releases or press conferences, and the paper misses stories, something local papers loathe, given the fierce competition among them (August 26).

In short, if they are to exercise the monitoring function, journalists cannot completely avoid upsetting the authorities, but at the same time have to be careful not to go too far. And in the age of the Internet and mobile devices, which have further eroded the establishment's power to manage the news, relationships between journalists and sources, newspapers and their subjects, the media and other institutions have become increasingly complex and delicate, mixing cooperation and conflict, dependence and resistance, friendship and enmity.

In addition, some journalists also see the internal references as a way of compromise. At least the message was conveyed to someone with the authorities, which provides some hope for making a difference. On this matter, Kunming journalists more or less share the view of journalists in other Chinese regions, as in one study in which 80% of the surveyed journalists agreed that "internal reporting serves as a watchdog function," and 67% agreed that "internal reporting can be more effective to solve problems" (Lin, 2010).

Undercover Reporting

Given the restricted environment, journalists who wish to accomplish their ideals, or sometimes simply to get the story, tend to hide their identity as a reporter while reporting. Unlike in the U.S., where deception in the quest of a news story is broadly considered a transgression in journalism, such means are widely condoned in Kunming. Among local investigative journalists, going undercover to get information is a fairly prevalent practice.

A longtime reporter, now an editor, described how he once pretended to be a relative of local people to investigate illegal gold mining on the Jinsha River. For three days, he stayed with a family close to the river and played the curious visitor while chatting with gold miners. Local people said the mining was controlled by mobs. "It was dangerous. I myself alone had to face a group of people, and those people all had hunting rifles," the reporter said. "After finishing the interviews, I felt cold sweat all over my body. Even my legs were collapsing" (October 18, I). He did get the story.

One investigative reporter said she has covered news covertly more often than overtly. "If you do not go undercover, you will get nothing," she said. "If you reveal your identity, again you will get nothing, and it will be dangerous." This reporter is not from Yunnan and does not speak the dialect. Speaking Mandarin, she often tells people that she is an investigator sent by the provincial government. In many places in Yunnan, where people seldom meet native Mandarin speakers, people generally believe her, she said (October 25).

Even when the issue at hand does not involve serious crimes or life-threatening danger, however, reporters sometimes playact. One day, I went with a reporter and a photographer to investigate vendors selling uncertified cosmetic contact lenses at a cartoon art fare—such lenses being popular among teenagers who like to dress up like comic book characters. After strolling along for quite a while, the reporter found an offending booth, peddling contacts in all kinds of bright colors that were immersed in some kind of liquid in small glass bottles. The reporter asked the price, just like a regular customer, and inquired why there were no labels on the bottles. The seller said the labels had been removed so people could see what was inside, and then showed us bottles with labels on, printed with Korean, saying the products were imported from Korea.

After the encounter, the reporter hid behind a giant advertisement board to scribble her notes. She never told anybody at the fair that she was a reporter. "For information that I can get as a customer, it is not necessary to reveal my identity as a reporter," said the reporter, adding that if she revealed her identity, people might be concerned about possible negative coverage and would tell less (August 19).

Reporters who use undercover methods, sometimes involving fooling others, see them as essential for getting people to divulge truthful information. "It is not nice to fool people," said one reporter, "but this is a working technique and does not violate professional ethics. It is permissible. Fooling people and undercover reporting are not matters of professional ethics, but are solutions driven by reality. American journalists can cover news with their identities revealed, but it cannot be done in China. Without undercover reporting, the truth of a story cannot be told" (September 13).

To summarize, realizing sweeping, society-wide changes are not feasible, many journalists tend to focus on the merits of gradual, small differences achieved through individual cases. "Change is too big a word," said one reporter, preferring "improve, and through individual cases, one after another," and added that this is a precondition for greater progress. "Without individual cases, there won't be [change in] the entire society" (October 13). The most satisfying experience for them is helping those in need, even though such actions are more in the realm of social charity rather than part of their job description. With the power of the press, the journalists were able to solve some problems for those who are deprived and disadvantaged, which gives the journalists a great sense of achievement. They are still frustrated, because their bigger dream of changing the whole system is not attainable and they know it. But the ability to help people in need one case at a time allows some journalists to find meaning in doing their job. They are still trying to achieve the bigger goals, hence the tactical handling of relations with the authorities and the widespread use of undercover reporting. They can also get some satisfaction out of these delicate practices, but helping the disadvantaged has become the main source for their sense of achievement as a journalist, therefore the main component of the tangible meaning of their job.

There are also those who give up the aspirations to avoid the frustrations and feeling conflicted, by either leaving journalism altogether or seeking alternatives. One chief editor, for example, is working toward distancing his paper from watchdog journalism, which used to be their selling point. He said it is simply too difficult to continue focusing on monitoring power because there is too much resistance. "Media monitoring ultimately means monitoring the government, otherwise the government will get even more reckless. Monitoring the government faces the biggest resistance" (October 18, II).

He is not alone. Not long before, a competing paper had gone through a makeover and come up with a new motto: "Make Life More Interesting." The newly hired chief editor at this reinvented paper said the new approach is to cover stories that appeal to both readers and the authorities, which in his view is not contradictory. " 'Interesting' means fun, making people happy after reading it," he said. He wants his paper to cover "people's little hobbies, little sadness, little pursuits, little dreams." As for loftier objectives, he said, "I do have journalistic ideals, but I won't say it. Meaningless to say it, because you can't achieve it, and what's the use of talking about it? You'll end up head broken and bleeding. What's the point?" (October 19, I).

After discussing these journalists' aspirations, frustrations, and reconciliations, the next question to ask is, Why? Where do the journalists get the aspirations? Why do they have to face so many constraints and end up so frustrated? And why do they use such particular ways of reconciling the discrepancy between what they wanted to achieve and what the reality allows them? To answer these questions, the aspirations, frustrations, and reconciliations already discussed need to be examined within the broader social and political context, which is the task of the next chapter.

References

Guo, M. (2011). 为什么是云信公益周刊 *[Why the public interest weekly in Yunxin]*. Retrieved February 15, 2012, from http://media.nfdaily.cn/cmyj/31/03/content/2011–09/06/content_29461310.htm

Lin, F. (2010). Organizational construction or individual's deed? The literati tradition in the journalistic professionalization in China. *International Journal of Communication, 4,* 175–197.

7 Journalism Culture in Context

Global Influence, Social Conflict, and Epidemic Mistrust

In exploring the journalism culture of metro papers in Kunming, the current study thus far has addressed local journalists' aspirations for their job, frustrations when their aspirations were not fully realized, and reconciliations that help render their job meaningful to them. These discussions touch upon two main aspects of the occupational culture of these journalists, cognitive (ideal, values, goals, assessment, etc.) and practical (behavior, practices), or the saying and the doing of these journalists. The researcher stresses that to fully understand the journalism culture of these metro paper journalists, the inquiry needs to examine the discrepancies between the saying and the doing, because it is precisely through such discrepancies that the probe can delve deeper. The result is a thick description (Geertz, 1973) of the journalism culture of this particular group of journalists that covers a broad range of reality as well as nuanced understanding.

However, journalism culture does not exist in a vacuum. Rather, it is deeply embedded in a social ambiance, perhaps even more so than some other occupations. With the goal of reaching a deeper and comprehensive understanding of Kunming's journalism culture, this chapter examines phenomena of the social, cultural environment that bear importantly on journalists' work. Given the complexity of any society's institutional and other macro-level constructs, I cannot possibly purport to address all the social and cultural elements that connect and interact with journalism. For instance, the Confucian literati tradition has been considered a major source of Chinese journalists' professional ideals of monitoring power and pushing for social change (Hassid, 2011; Lin, 2010; Pan & Lu, 2003), but will not be the focus of this discussion. Rather, this chapter highlights several aspects of the social and cultural environment that emerged from my fieldwork as particularly relevant to the journalism culture under investigation.

Global Influence

The term "overseas" (*guo wai*), which in regular Chinese parlance refers to developed, democratic Western countries and occasionally advanced industrial countries in Asia such as Japan and Korea, came up frequently in journalists' conversations and in my interviews. It was such a prominent pattern in my conversation with the journalists as well as amongst themselves that it almost seemed like no conversation was complete until such comparisons were made. A journalist was groaning in front of his computer one day when he saw stories authored by his colleagues were posted on Yunnan Net, the portal of the provincial Party organ *Yunnan Daily*, without crediting his own paper as the origin. "Bestseller writers in the U.S. can buy a big house in New York City. Not gonna happen in China. China doesn't protect the cultural industry, writers or intellectual property" was his conclusion (October 11, II). Another day, during a lunch break in the newsroom, the journalists had an impromptu conversation about Steve Jobs, who died just a few days before. The conversation soon changed from admiring Jobs to inquiring why China did not have its own Steve Jobs, whereby the journalists condemned China's rigid educational methods, the convention of looking down upon people without a college degree, and the culture of suppressing and punishing kids who think and act differently from others (October 8, II). In other words, the conversation turned into a comparison between China and the U.S., with the conclusion that China lags behind the U.S. in terms of innovation and creativity.

In indeed, in such comparisons, China usually is deemed inferior to other countries, especially the U.S., from small things such as drinkable tap water to big issues like press freedom, political systems, and the conduct of government officials. In July 2011, for example, Chinese media paid fervent attention to the new U.S. Ambassador to China Gary Locke when he first arrived in China, noting admiringly that he flew coach and ate simply. A chief editor explained this as a reflection of Chinese people's dislike of government officials and general antipathy toward those with means. "In China, government officials are the privileged stratus, which leads to hatred toward the powerful and the rich," he said. "Americans do not hate the rich. They respect people who build something from nothing. Many rich people in China made their wealth through illegal approaches and collusion with the authorities. Therefore in China, wealth is a sensitive topic" (October 18, II).

Kunming journalists frequently mention *The New York Times*, and even the *Huffington Post*, as representing higher standards of journalism than China's media provide, all the while admiring Western media's freedom, something Chinese media lack. "Media in China are totally controlled by a political party. Foreign media, although more or less influenced by political parties, feel like independent institutions," one executive commented (September 21). Another journalist asserted that the U.S. muckrakers of the olden days faced far less dire conditions than do China's investigative journalists today.

These metro paper journalists admitted having borrowed a lot of American journalism ideas to form their own journalistic values. One chief editor said, "Metro papers are the typical example of the mixture of Chinese and American values" (September 13). To him, the American part includes being a watchdog, speaking for the people, and promoting basic human rights, which, as already discussed, is part of their aspiration, whereas the Chinese part emphasizes the legitimacy of the authorities and virtues of social stability.

The biggest American idea that they borrow, perhaps, is "universal values," deemed a very sensitive topic by the Kunming journalists. At one meeting I attended, a chief editor first told his editors and executives not to use the term freely, because Chinese leaders would deem it the "spread of American values." But then he continued,

> The core of universal values is the guarantee of people's basic rights. China's problem is lack of guarantee for people's basic rights. The Party does not mention universal values, because mentioning it means to share power and interests with the people. Lack of universal values leads to hatred toward the authorities and the rich.

But he reiterated that journalists should be "cautious" in using the term, adding, "This is the red line." A small paper in Southwest China that is not a major player on China's political stage should be all the more restrained about promoting ideas like universal values, he said, but added that, "Local news needs to show some values," just not to label them as "universal values" (September 13). Apparently, these Kunming journalists considered "universal values" an American idea that provides the blueprint of what a good society is supposed to have, and what they aspire China to have.

The salience of American values further emerged in coverage of the 10th anniversary of the September 11 terrorist attacks, when many Chinese newspapers published special supplements to commemorate the occasion. All four local metros published an insert of around 16 pages with color photos, fancy graphics, and lengthy stories, many translations from U.S. media, with accounts of or about victims, survivors, and families as well as commentary and analysis from American journalists, politicians, experts, and so on. As such, these supplements largely consisted of American stories, emotions, and points of view. No wonder one chief editor called the local coverage of the anniversary "more American than America."

"The 9.11 coverage is a bizarre product of China's media," added this editor. "We do not care about our own stuff, and are not allowed to care. This kind of environment pushes Chinese media toward American values." He mentioned *The Glory and the Dream: A Narrative History of America, 1932–1972*, by William Manchester, saying every single chief editor at Kunming metro papers has a copy of the Chinese edition, published in 2006. "Metro papers . . . want to distance themselves from Party organs, are resistant to government requests, and admire the media environment in the U.S.," he said (October 18, II).

Such collective perception of an often-superior system abroad provides a comparative framework these journalists use to evaluate social reality in China and the performance of Chinese institutions and authorities. Western countries and their media, however vague or mythical they may be in Chinese people's minds, are upheld as the standard or ideal, thus becoming a source of aspiration (i.e., what things are supposed to be).

The flip side of an ideal *guo wai* (overseas) is precisely a disappointing *guo nei* (domestic). The catch phrase, "Chinese characteristics," which the government has held as a fundamental principal, as in "building the socialism with Chinese characteristics," has become something of a joke in the public eye. People use the term mockingly in reference to a wide range of negative social phenomena in China, from government corruption, food adulteration, and counterfeit products to suppression of expression. Comparison of political systems between China and Western countries often aggravates journalists' dissatisfaction with the Chinese government, thus contributing to their frustration. A young reporter told me:

> In this country, under such a system, the government's attitude in dealing with disasters will be unsatisfactory. During the Wenzhou train collision, [the government decided to] bury the train cars on the site. Compare with how Britain and France handled [similar train collisions in their countries], how they searched for bodies and handled belongings of the victims; how Japan searched for bodies and handled belongings of the victims after the tsunami [in 2011]. It has been 10 years since 9.11, but the U.S. is still searching for and identifying victims. The Chinese government just tried to get it over with as soon as possible, forcing victim's families to sign [compensation agreements].
>
> (September 21)

An investigative journalist told me about reporting on heavy pollution emitted by a chemical plant built near Dianchi Lake, a large freshwater lake whose water quality has been severely degraded in recent decades. The plant owner was a Korean businessman, and the reporter asked what his government would do if a highly polluting chemical plant was built near a major lake in Korea. The owner told her those responsible would face criminal charges and heavy sentences. Yet in Kunming, his chemical plant is allowed to operate near a lake whose pollution the government has been trying to clean up. "What was our government thinking? I don't know," the reporter said (September 26, II).

Journalists are mostly gloomy about how China stacks up, but their disappointment and dissatisfaction also help motivate their desire for change. As such, global influences became an important ingredient in the mix of aspiration and frustration.

Social Conflict

The environment within which Kunming journalists operate is fraught with social conflict, especially that between the powerful and powerless. Below, I offer two scenarios from my experiences accompanying reporters.

During the wee hours of October 7, 2011, in a small town on the outskirts of Kunming that was changing from a rural village into a suburb, two teenage boys were suddenly attacked by a group of about 40 men wearing security guard uniforms and wielding steel pipes and wooden sticks. The boys, said to be cousins, had stopped at a small restaurant for a snack following a birthday party they'd attended at a nearby karaoke club (KTV). One of them, a 17-year-old high school student, suffered severe injuries and died soon after being sent to the hospital. The next day, the victim's father set up a memorial for his son in front of the gate of the township government, demanding explanation. Photos of the memorial circulated on Weibo and soon drew the attention of local reporters. The security guards were said to be working for the local government, which first said the uniformed men had confused the boys with others, but later refused to confirm that statement, citing ongoing police investigation. The township government subsequently told the press the men were security guards hired through an agency.

The following day, I accompanied a reporter going back to the town seeking more details. We paid a visit to the victim's home in a nearby village. It was a newly built two-story house, nicely furnished. The boy's father, a skinny, tall, country man in his 50s, looked drained and emotionless. He had lost his only child. A huge framed black-and-white photograph of the victim, the typical funeral portrait, stood in a corner of the living room. Two young girls were folding paper money into the shape of silver ingots, hundreds of them, which were to be burnt in front of the photo, a traditional way of mourning the dead. A woman reporter from another local paper was there as well.

Two more cousins, also young men, were paying a visit to the family, and we all sat on plastic stools in a circle in the backyard and talked. The reporters discreetly but openly recorded the conversation with iPhones and occasionally took notes. The cousins voiced dissatisfaction toward the township government, criticizing local officials as trying to avoid responsibility. They insisted that the uniformed men were actually *cheng guan*, or city patrol officers, not contracted outside security guards. Exactly who had killed the teenager that night, city patrol or security guards, was never clarified in this incident. Hired security were said to often assist city patrol, which only made things more confusing.

City patrol forces (see also Chapter 6 of this volume) have been a hot spot of social conflict in China, because they typically are the ones who demolish old homes to make way for new construction projects, chase away farmers trying to sell homegrown produce in the city streets without permits, and otherwise brutalize ordinary citizens. The victim's cousins had quite some stories to tell about how local city patrol bullied people. In one case, they said, city patrol had forcibly torn down one of their homes. Later they ran into the captain of the force, and the captain baldly admitted to the demolition, with a what-can-you-do-about-me attitude. As one of the young men was trying to take a cellphone picture of him, the captain warned, "Young man, you're still young. You need to think it through." The cousins saw this as basically a death threat. Based on such experiences, they were convinced that city patrol were the real culprits in the killing of their cousin (October 10, II). By the end of 2011, the father of the victim was still waiting for justice.

In another case, one Friday morning, after repeated hotline calls to the newsroom, a reporter got an assignment to cover a protest by a group of migrant workers demanding back pay. The reporter arrived at Yunnan Road and Bridge Corp Ltd., a construction company and site of the protest. The steel gate at the entrance was ostensibly closed, but with one corner bent back to create a two-foot gap where people could crouch through—the migrant workers themselves had made the opening after the company had locked them out. A glass door behind the steel gate was broken. The reporter and I crouched underneath the bent steel gate and went inside. In the lobby, a coffee table was turned upside down, with glass from a tabletop scattered everywhere, and several broken flowerpots along with flowers rooted in soil lay on the floor. Alongside the mess, sitting quietly around a huge oval table and smoking, were representatives of the migrant workers, waiting to talk to leaders from the company.

The reporter interviewed one representative, who said a worker in his 60s had been beaten up by company thugs earlier that day and was now in a nearby hospital. He said the construction company owed millions of yuan in wages for a highway construction project finished a few months before, and that this was the second day they had come to ask for the payment, bringing along about 200 migrant workers to protest, after the company had failed to respond to repeated requests earlier. Asked why they were not going to higher authorities, another representative said this company had people coming to ask for back pay every single day, and some of the cases had been before the authorities for years but had yet to be resolved. "How is it possible that we can wait? School is starting in a few days," he said. Many of the migrant workers needed money to pay for their children's tuition and fees. They all spoke the dialect of Chongqing, a city about 550 miles from Kunming.

That afternoon, the reporter I was with paid a visit to the injured migrant worker in the hospital. We found the 61-year-old man in the emergency room, sitting on a wheeled stretcher with an IV hooked up, groaning and vomiting. His face was covered with bruises and scrapes, with a swollen bump on his forehead. The doctor said he had suffered a concussion and needed to be hospitalized, so he was about to be transferred to a patient room. The man said he had worked on road construction for about eight months and received not a penny in payment, except for free meals. His wife said they needed money for a grandchild's schooling because the child's father, their son, was too ill to work. Like most of the protesting migrant workers, this couple was from Chongqing. The man said staffers from the company had grabbed him and beaten him up as he was coming out of a restroom, and his wife found him lying on the floor bleeding, whereupon fellow workers got him to the hospital.

The reporter helped push the man's stretcher to another building, where he was settled into a room with three other patients. Outside the room, the reporter talked with the man's niece, who had come to the protest to support her uncle. She showed us scratches on her arm and chest, saying some female staffers from the construction company had cursed her, called her names, and attacked her while she was standing at the door of their office. "We are all farmers. Those people are just mistreating our farmers," the woman said tearfully.

Later in the afternoon, when we were back at the demonstration site, the company sent someone to negotiate with the migrant workers and promised to pay back wages in a few days. This wasn't the first time this reporter had covered migrant workers protesting for back pay. "Many companies in China do not have credibility," he said, and owing back payments to workers were commonplace (August 26).

In short, Chinese journalists nowadays cannot avoid social conflict all around them. Their frequent encounters with social conflict are in line with the dramatic rise of such conflict in general in Chinese society. After more than three decades of economic development, and despite overall rising living standards, the gap between the haves and have-nots in China has grown alarmingly. Widespread corruption among government and Party officials simply aggravates the disparities. The growing unhappiness among China's dispossessed is evident in rising incidence of protest. In 2003, the government reported 58,000 "mass incidents," and in 2005 the number rose to 74,000 (Guo & Guo, 2008). In a recent survey, the Chinese public expressed growing concerns over inequality and corruption (Pew Research Center, 2012). In today's China, new patterns of exclusion and inclusion are forming along the lines of class, ethnicity, region, and the urban–rural division. An alliance among political, economic, and intellectual elites has concentrated the greatest rewards of the reforms in the hands of a small group of people, leaving many struggling, grieving, and sometimes, protesting (Zhao, 2008).

The prevalence of social conflict gives many journalists serious pause about the well-being of Chinese society. One veteran said, "It feels that media monitoring lags far behind the society's decline." He thinks suppression and exploitation by the powerful against the common people has been worsening (September 18). Such concerns are a driving force for journalists' aspirations to monitor power, plead for the people, and make a difference through news coverage. The sheer fact of so many powerless people needing help has cultivated a sense of advocacy among not just journalists in Kunming, but also in other places of China, as shown by other research (Bai, 2012). Such advocacy has clear value judgment: advocate for people of the lower strata of the society, push for social advance, and emphasize public interests and social justice (Bai, 2012). When journalists' advocacy does not change things much, however, they feel profound frustration. But when their advocacy turns into real impact, even in small ways, as documented in Chapter 6 of this volume, journalists get a sense of achievement and fulfillment, which reconciles with their inability to make grand changes to the entire society.

The Pandemic of Mistrust

Another salient social condition that these journalists deal with on a daily basis is the widespread mistrust—lack of trust between individuals, as well as between individuals and public institutions. Such mistrust has become endemic across Chinese society and reached an alarming level. Journalists themselves are also mistrusting and being mistrusted.

Mistrust Between Common People and the Authorities

A reporter followed up a lead from a candidate for a government post who had passed a written exam and interview but been disqualified after a physical, the last step in the recruiting process. The reporter conducted an interview with an official at the government recruiting office, who seemed candid in her responses. She showed documents indicating the candidate had kidney problems and did not meet government health standards for new recruits. The reporter told the official that some people thought perhaps the applicant did not have the correct *guanxi*, or connections, and lost his opportunity to someone who did. The official laughed and went on to explain the recruiting process, emphasizing that there was little room for cheating. The reporter continued to mention the element of mistrust, whereas the official claimed there was no hanky-panky. "The health standard is there, the process is open and transparent, and there is no foul play in any single step. [The scenario of] disqualifying one person in order to save the spot for another does not exist," the official said (September 16). But without the mistrust-driven assumptions of foul play, the reporter would not have followed up the applicant's suspicions in the first place.

In another case, a family blaming a hospital for a patient's death resulted in additional hospitalization—the wife and son had encountered a hospital staff member in a park, a fight had broken out, and the son and mother had ended up in the very hospital that they claimed had mistreated and killed their father and husband.

A tipster gave the information to a reporter whom I accompanied to the hospital, where we met with the vice president who acted as the spokesman. The hospital official spoke in tough and serious tone, starting by mentioning several well-publicized incidents around the country in which patients or their families who claimed to have been mistreated beat up or even killed physicians. He said media coverage of similar events could only lend more ammunition to angry patients and encourage more harm to medical practitioners. More than once, he said, "We recommend that you do not cover this incident." He then accused the son and mother of starting the fight, saying his employee was the victim of two unreasonable, angry family members of a former patient whose death had nothing to do with his hospital. He particularly described the son as antigovernment, violent, and vicious, saying, "He is 40-something, jobless, divorced. His income is just his parents' retirement salary."

We next visited the son and mother on a ward a few floors below the spokesman's office. The mother was lying on a bed, eyes shut. The son soon walked in. He said he was "self-employed," and that he walked with his mother every Saturday in the park where the fight took place. The mother said the hospital worker had started it, that the worker's wife pushed her down to the ground and stomped on her chest a couple of times, and that when her son came over to stop the wife, he got into a fight with the husband. A shirt stained with blood was taped to the wall above the son's hospital bed. The mother said she planned to transfer to another hospital for treatment because she could not trust people in this hospital (September 26).

The vast majority of hospitals in China are run by the government, and therefore can be seen as an extension of the authorities. In recent years, there have been numerous cases where angry patients or family members blocked the hospital gate, displayed the dead body of a loved one allegedly mistreated in the hospital, or threatened to jump off the hospital building. In extreme cases, angry relatives of patients even physically attack or kill the doctors. This kind of incident has become so common that people have given it a term, *yi nao*, or "hospital disturbance" (Tu, 2014). *Yi nao* is a typical example of common people's mistrust toward public institutions such as hospitals. They stage this kind of disturbance because they do not trust that death or injuries occurring during hospitalization are simply medical accidents; they'd rather believe they are caused by deliberation or negligence, because the doctors only care about how much bribe money they can get from the patients rather than the latter's well-being. People also have little confidence that their grievance can be addressed fairly by the hospital and therefore resort to drastic measures to express anger and frustration, as well as seeking compensation.

Mistrust between common people and the authorities also played a big role in both the case of the teenager beaten to death by security guards and the migrant workers seeking back pay. The teenager's father had set up a memorial at the local government offices to make a scene and attract media attention, because he did not trust the government to take the issue seriously without some media exposure (October 11, II). As for the two cousins who talked with reporters later, their mistrust toward the local government was only too obvious.

In the migrant worker case, the road and bridge construction company, said to have close ties with the government, had breached the workers' trust when it failed to pay wages guaranteed by contract. The workers did not trust the company itself, or labor authorities, to redress the wrong and thus turned to protest. When company thugs beat up a worker, other workers naturally did not trust the police officer who arrived to investigate. A protest leader, automatically assuming the officer would side with the company, accused her of receiving a 20,000-yuan payoff from the company, which the officer denied fervently. Still, protesters continued to complain to the officer that she was not on the side of the people, although her salary came from the people's tax money. The officer insisted that she was just doing her job, without favoring any side, and that she actually sympathized with the workers and thought they had the right to request their pay (August 26).

Mistrust Between Journalists and Authorities

In the teenager's case, one reporter covering the story called the government response "nonsense," observing that the press conference ostensibly held to explain the beating lasted only five minutes, and consisted of local officials reading a press release but taking no questions. "For things like this, [the government] should shoulder whatever responsibility it should shoulder, deal with it with due process. The government is always trying to evade its responsibility and therefore has lost public trust," the reporter said (October 10, II).

Also, the reporter who covered the migrant worker protest had mistrust toward the company, which he said had close ties with the local government. He said if the company knew a reporter was there, they could phone their connections within the local government, which in turn might put pressure on his newspaper to kill the story. So the reporter did not identify himself to the company executive present at the negotiations, essentially going undercover. He did not even ask for a business card from the executive or obtain the executive's full name, and used only his surname in the story (August 26).

Indeed, journalists' suspicions toward authorities drive the common practice of undercover reporting among metro paper journalists in Kunming, as well as other places in China. Journalists covering sensitive stories often anticipate that if they try to obtain information openly, authorities will intervene, sometimes forcefully, or sources will lie for fear of punishment. The authorities, on the other hand, have little trust in journalists, often seeing them as adversaries—even though a great deal of the reporting about officials and official matters is positive.

An investigative reporter told me about going to a rural town to investigate two teenagers' deaths in a coal mine. Local officials told them the two teenagers had entered the mine by themselves and suffocated, and the deaths were an accident. The reporter and photographer then insisted on going to the boys' home village about a 10-kilometer walk away, and the local officials followed them. She and her colleague finally threw off their tail by walking faster, and reached the teenagers' homes at about 10:30 that night. The family confirmed that the teenagers had gone to explore the coal mine by themselves, and said the government already had offered them compensation.

At around 1:00 in the morning, local government officials invited the two journalists for a very late dinner, after which one official summoned the reporter to an office upstairs and gave her a thick envelope. "I estimated there was 10,000 to 20,000 yuan in it," the reporter said. She called the photographer up to join her, and both refused the money. "I told them I cannot accept this kind of money that involves death," the reporter said. She knew the officials were worried about their image, and she told them to "please trust our ethics and morality." The township officials nevertheless were upset at the rejection and immediately had the journalists driven to the county seat, which oversees the township. The next day, the county Party secretary invited the two journalists to a meal and explained that officials in that locality had not seen a reporter for many years and were afraid the coverage would cost them their positions (October 25). Clearly, the township government officials had little faith in the integrity of news media and journalists.

Similar fears underlie the common practice among government officials of giving only a family name when answering journalists' questions, for the fear of being named in "bad stories." Kunming metro papers thus are full of references to sources such as Mr. Zhang or Ms. Wang. Many stories also use anonymous sources, vague mentions of locations, and other blurred facts. One reporter said he uses people's full names about half the time (September 23, I). Another said most of the time he uses only surnames, usually at sources' request (October 8, II).

Mistrust Between Journalists and the Disadvantaged

Lack of trust even pervades journalists' attitudes toward the very groups they typically try to help. "You cannot trust people blindly," said an editor. "Chinese people are too smart and have too many tricks. Some people may use your sympathy. So you need to learn to discern and be a smart journalist" (September21). Indeed, many of his colleagues related experiences of being misled by the very people with whom they sympathized.

One reporter described her disappointment with a man who had asked for help in a dispute with a hospital. "I felt the patient was very pitiable. My heart softened," she said. The story was published, and the next day, the hospital labeled it fabrication and phoned the reporter repeatedly to curse and threaten her. She had gone to the hospital twice during her reporting and officials there had refused to do interviews. She had not recorded her interviews. And now the patient was nowhere to be found anymore and no one could back up her story. "My editor speculated that the hospital had given some money to the patient for him to keep his mouth shut. His purpose was just money," the reporter said. "This incident chilled my heart. That patient, I thought he was so pitiable, so disadvantaged, but once he reached his objective, he kicked me away" (September 27, II).

Thus results a triangle of mistrust: Common folks, including disadvantaged people, think "journalists can do more than authorities," a veteran reporter said (October 16). Their mistrust toward government officials and other authorities is often what drives them to seek help from the media, especially market-oriented outlets like the metro papers. Journalists at these outlets usually have little faith in the authorities, sharing the public perceptions to a degree.

The authorities, in turn, doubt journalists, regarding them as antigovernment crusaders or corruptible individuals who care more about money than ethics and integrity—and in fact, past reports about journalists taking bribes from sources seeking positive coverage have hurt the occupation's reputation (Zha, 1995, 1998), although I did not observe or learn of such practices in the context of my fieldwork. Journalists also have become wary of common folks who plead with them for help, although generally speaking, journalists are more ready to suspect the authorities than they do the common folks. Journalists thus operate in the authorities–common people (including disadvantaged group)–journalists triangle. Mistrust resides on each pair of relationships (see Figure 7.1). More often than not, such pandemic mistrust is a major contributing factor to the obstacles facing the journalists, hence their frustration.

As with social conflicts, mistrust has become so entrenched in Chinese society that it is almost part of the air the journalists breathe, and therefore deserves further probing. Trust in systems or institutions may be understood as confidence or faith in the reliability of the systems or institutions to work the way they are supposed to and deliver desirable outcomes (Giddens, 1990; Li, 2004). People are likely to trust and think positively about the state or public institutions that perform as expected (Mishler & Rose, 2001; Yang & Tang, 2010). When their performance has fallen short of public expectations, public trust toward authorities and institutions are low. This is the case in China.

A landmark case of Chinese society's trust crisis is the so-called Guo Meimei controversy, which raged across the Internet and in the news media in mid-2011. The 19-year-old Guo Meimei, a young woman whose mother had made a fortune through stock trading, boasted on Weibo about her wealth, with photos of her luxury cars, top brand handbags, and much else, and identified herself as an administrator for the Red Cross Society of China. Outrage spread through Weibo reposts and comments, with people interpreting her extravagant lifestyle as evidence of corruption in the Red Cross. There had been corruption cases of the organization over the years and people were already losing trust in it. As it turned out, Guo had no real association with the organization. She said she had claimed the affiliation

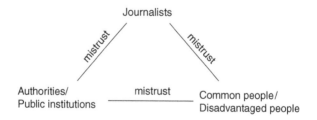

Figure 7.1 The Triangle of Mistrust

out of vanity (Wang & Chen, 2011). But by then, her online bragging and lying had thoroughly undermined public trust in the Red Cross, and donations to the organization plunged (Beijing Morning Post, 2012).

The most noteworthy aspect of this episode, I argue, is that all the criticism focused not on the bored, vain rich girl herself. Rather, people assumed her claims were true and directed their anger and denunciations at the Red Cross. In other words, people chose to give credit to a teenager out of nowhere over a 100-year-old, well-known, state-sanctioned national organization. Or, the public was not so much willing to believe a young woman as ready to doubt a state-sponsored institution. This controversy was not just about the Red Cross, but exposed Chinese public's long-held, staggering mistrust and dissatisfaction toward the entire state apparatus.

Such mistrust has not gotten any better as time goes by. In March 2016, a Shanghai-based digital native news service, The Paper (www.thepaper.cn), published a story about vaccines not properly refrigerated and becoming useless or even harmful being sold across 18 provinces and cities in China (The Paper, 2016). These vaccines were not government-mandated, the most essential vaccines, but the public was still shocked. The story soon went viral on social media and triggered a public outcry. Citizens, parents, and experts all chimed in to post articles on WeChat, China's rising social media platform (see Chapter 8 of this volume), expressing anger, panic, and of course, mistrust. People's mistrust were targeted at the authorities, namely, government agencies supervising the distribution and use of vaccines. "How horrible is this! If even the government's disease control department and vaccination agencies are not trustworthy, then for us common people, facing vaccines that we know nothing about, what can we trust?" asked one mother (Mengya Institute, 2016). Many people were especially angry over the fact that the people who sold these vaccines had been doing that for five years before they were caught in 2015, based on the article by The Paper (The Paper, 2016). "This kind of vaccine problems could only cause more parents to lose confidence in vaccines in China, leading to more unimmunized children. Such an appalling crime lasted five years before it was discovered. I don't know what the authorities have been doing?" Wrote a pediatrician (Pei, 2016). There were also parents posting on WeChat expressing mistrust of public hospitals, where people unusually will go to get vaccines, and considering going to private health care providers, which are usually much more expensive (March 2016, personal communication).

In sum, global influence, social conflict, and mistrust are three most salient aspects of the social environment of these journalists, as observed through my field study. They are the social conditions that the journalists deal with day in and day out, shaping both their perception and practice, contributing to their aspirations, frustrations, and reconciliations. Another important element of the social environment is technology, especially social media, which will be examined in detail in the next chapter.

References

Bai, H. (2012). 从倡导到中立：当代中国调查记者的职业角色变迁 [From initiative to neutrality: Changes in the professional roles of investigative journalists in contemporary China]. 新闻记者 *[Journalism Review]*, 2.

Beijing Morning Post. (2012). 中国红十字会决定撤销商红会 *[China Red Cross decided to cancel its commerce branch]*. Retrieved March 28, 2012, from http://news.sina.com.cn/c/2012–01–01/011923732954.shtml

Geertz, C. (1973). *The interpretation of cultures: Selected essays*. New York: Basic Books.

Giddens, A. (1990). *The consequences of modernity*. Stanford, CA: Stanford University Press.

Guo, B., & Guo, S. (2008). China in search of a harmonious society. In S. Guo (Ed.), *China in search of a harmonious society* (pp. 1–12). Plymouth, UK: Lexington Books.

Hassid, J. (2011). Four models of the fourth estate: A typology of contemporary Chinese journalists. *China Quarterly, 208*, 813–832.

Li, L. (2004). Political trust in rural China. *Modern China, 30*(2), 228–258.

Lin, F. (2010). Organizational construction or individual's deed? The literati tradition in the journalistic professionalization in China. *International Journal of Communication, 4*, 175–197.

Mengya Institute. (2016, March 23). "黑疫苗"事件爆出来之后，一个妈妈的提问 [After "black vaccine" incident revealed, a mother's questioning]. Message posted to http://mp.weixin.qq.com/s?__biz=MzA5NjUwOTYwOA==&mid=405468919&idx=1&sn=2928f38740ad3121d4c5ea73ae2334ba&scene=5&srcid=0323djUD2tmqg6lqBCiN2Oaf#rd

Mishler, W., & Rose, R. (2001). What are the origins of political trust? Testing institutional and cultural theories in post-communist societies. *Comparative Political Studies, 34*(1), 30–62.

Pan, Z., & Lu, Y. (2003). Localizing professionalism: Discursive practices in China's media reforms. In C. Lee (Ed.), *Chinese media, global contexts* (pp. 215–236). London: Routledge.

The Paper. (2016, March 18). 数亿元劣质疫苗流入18省份，是危害全社会的恐怖事件 [Hundreds of millions of dollars' worth of poor quality vaccines distributed to 18 provinces and cities is a horrible incident that harms the society]. Message posted to http://mp.weixin.qq.com/s?__biz=MzA4MzI3OTUxMg==&mid=404857926&idx=1&sn=9a12ba7e927b96b28a66103a452964e0&scene=5&srcid=0504QLCQW3sEwrmgLh4Zx9jC#rd

Pei, H. (2016, March 18). 面对问题疫苗，我们怎么办 [Facing problematic vaccines, what should we do]? Message posted to http://mp.weixin.qq.com/s?__biz=

MzA5NzE5ODIyOQ==&mid=403308367&idx=1&sn=664e0a04a4fc84f5c4432
e3d78484e89&scene=5&srcid=031884jjOcA4cSg95rvjiwBg#rd
Pew Research Center. (2012). *Growing concerns in China about inequality, corruption.* Retrieved October 26, 2012, from http://www.pewglobal.org/2012/10/16/
growing-concerns-in-china-about-inequality-corruption/
Tu, J. (2014). Yinao: Protest and violence in China's medical sector. *Berkeley Journal of Sociology.* Retrieved on May 5, 2016, from http://berkeleyjournal.
org/2014/12/yinao-protest-and-violence-in-chinas-medical-sector/
Wang, Y., & Chen, Y. (2011). 郭美美携母接受郎咸平专访 撇清与红十字会关系 *[Guo Meimei and mom talk with Liang Xianping, denying relationship with Red Cross].* Retrieved August 4, 2011, from http://news.qq.com/a/20110804/000246.
htm?pgv_ref=aio
Yang, Q., & Tang, W. (2010). Exploring the sources of institutional trust in China: Culture, mobilization, or performance? *Asian Politics and Policy, 2*(3), 415–436.
Zha, J. (1995). *China pop: How soap operas, tabloids, and bestsellers are transforming a culture.* New York: New Press.
Zhao, Y. (1998). *Media, market, and democracy in China: Between the party line and the bottom line.* Urbana, IL: University of Illinois Press.
Zhao, Y. (2008). *Communication in China: Political economy, power, and conflict.* Lanham, MD: Rowman & Littlefield.

8 Social Media Impact

The first advice a deputy chief editor of a Kunming metro paper gave to me, during our very first meeting, was to open a Weibo account (July 19). I did a few days later and discovered a whole new world of these journalists (see Chapter 2 of this volume for background information on Weibo).

Nearly every single reporter or editor I interacted with had a Weibo account, and they checked their accounts incessantly—during meetings, while waiting to be served at a restaurant, or sitting in a karaoke club listening to colleagues belt their lungs out. As China's burgeoning social media at that time, Weibo provided the journalists a fresh and striking experience of the power of sharing, something the predecessor of weibo, Internet BBS, didn't quite possess. Together with the prevalence of mobile phones and 4G network, social media, such as Weibo, and recently WeChat, have become pivotal in changing the way journalists work, particularly in terms of pushing the boundaries of media coverage in the carefully controlled press system.

Based on my observation, there are five ways through which social media enable journalists to push the boundaries of their practice. First, social media provide new sources of information and more channels to discover story ideas. Information in China is often tightly controlled. Without social media, many of the stories or topics are easily buried. Second, social media broaden the range of public discourse to include topics eschewed by conventional media. Third, social media provide additional channels for news dissemination and therefore enable journalists to defy censorship. For example, reporters can break news swiftly on Weibo, before the authorities can even react or issue a story ban (Repnikova, 2014). Fourth, social media have the potential to go viral and therefore the ability to generate, sometimes surprisingly, bigger impact than relying on regular news distribution alone, even if the postings were short lived. Fifth, social media like Weibo also allow journalists more opportunities to interact with government officials, such as using the @ function, and force the government to be more transparent to some degree. Normally in China, it is very difficult for journalists to get in touch with government officials. Phone calls are often unanswered, face-to-face interviews rare, and interview requests often ignored. But if the officials have a Weibo account, which many of them do, they expose themselves on social media and sometimes have to react to inquiries of the public or the press.

This chapter addresses these five scenarios in detail and discusses the remaining limitations, despite the power of social media. But first, it is helpful to examine a prominent case that illustrated the impact of Weibo on journalism.

Weibo's Impact on Journalism Amid the Wenzhou Train Collision

A couple of weeks after I started my fieldwork, on the night of July 23, 2011, a high-speed train collided into the rear of another near the city of Wenzhou, in the coastal province of Zhejiang. Together, these two trains were carrying more than 1,000 passengers. Several cars derailed and plunged off the viaduct, hitting the ground; one was left dangling over the bridge. At least 40 people were killed in the accident, and hundreds more injured (Wines & LaFraniere, 2011).

Going simply by casualties, the 7.23 train collision was not the most horrific accident in China's recent history, but its social impact was enormous (Osnos, 2012). And the role of social media proved pivotal in this episode, for it was the microblog service Sina Weibo that transformed the occasion into a public crusade against the negligence, arrogance, and dishonesty of the Chinese government, particularly the powerful Railway Ministry. For the Chinese press, Kunming metro papers included, the experience affirmed how important new technologies, especially social media, have become in the conduct of journalism.

In fact, Weibo took the stage even before the accident occurred. Seven minutes before the crash, a Weibo user on one of the trains posted about the thunderstorm and said the train was "crawling more slowly than a snail" (Bao, 2011). Four minutes after the collision, a passenger on the train that ran into the rear of the other sent out the first word of the collision via Weibo: "D301 had an accident in Wenzhou. Suddenly stopped, with strong strike. Twice! All power is out!" This post appeared on the Internet two hours before the first breaking news item on the collision released by mainstream news media (Xinhua Net, 2011). Meanwhile, Weibo posts calling for help, seeking information about passengers, updating the situation on the scene, and so on were flooding Sina Weibo.

In the days following the collision, more and more people—common folks, victims, families, scholars, journalists, celebrities—chimed in and expanded the discourse to question the cause of the accident, criticize the government responses, praise Wenzhou volunteers helping with the rescue efforts, speculate about corruption, and cast doubts over China's entire development strategy. By noon of July 24, the number of Weibo posts about the accident on Sina Weibo surpassed 3 million and counting (Xinhua Net, 2011).

One of the most widely circulated posts came from columnist Tong Dahuan, whose plea has become the classic statement of the collision's core significance: "China, please go a little more slowly. Please stop your running steps, wait for your people, wait for your soul, wait for your morality, and wait for your conscience. Do not let trains derail, bridges collapse, roads turn into traps, buildings become dangerous. Go a bit slowly, and allow every life to have freedom and dignity, every person not to be left behind by this era, and everybody to reach their destination safely." Within 24 hours, this post was reposted more than 280,000 times and drew more than 30,000 additional comments (Tong, 2011). It was also quoted in a *New York Times* story on the collision (Johnson, 2011).

Journalists at Kunming metro papers, like journalists around the country, were watching closely the Weibo commotion over the collision. Two days after the collision, at a regular editorial meeting in one of the Kunming newsrooms I was observing, the chief editor gave a lecture to his staff, using a PowerPoint presentation titled "Behind the News: Weibo's Push." I attended many such meetings at this paper throughout my fieldwork, and this was the only time that I saw the chief editor do such a formal talk. During his lecture, he identified and discussed five dimensions of Weibo's impact on the press coverage: speed (*sudu*), temperature (*wendu*), attitude (*taidu*), range (*guangdu*), and depth (*shendu*). Following are the key points of the chief editor's talk regarding the five dimensions.

Weibo demonstrated stunning speed by breaking the news two hours ahead of the rest of news media. After learning about the accident on Weibo, thousands of Wenzhou people flocked to the scene and waited in line in the summer heat to have their blood drawn at donation stations. Locals who came to the rescue before the troops arrived took the injured to hospitals in their own vehicles, showing the warmth of people's heart. While China Central Television's (CCTV) coverage of the response was mostly about the troops and government reactions, local people's initiative deserved the limelight, said the chief editor, "This is the light of humanity, the warmth of Wenzhou people, and the hope of China, not the troops, not the Zhejiang government, not Hu-Wen," he said—the latter being a reference to the then central leaders, Hu Jintao and Wen Jiabao.

The chief editor then showed a widely circulated Weibo photo juxtaposing the front pages of four major Party newspapers on July 24, the day after the accident, with that of *Southern Metropolis Daily*, a market-oriented tabloid in Guangzhou. The Party organs—*People's Daily*, *Guangming Daily*, *Economic Daily*, and *People's Liberation Army Daily*—look nearly identical and have the same lead story and photo, about a Central Military Commission ceremony honoring newly promoted generals. Not a word about the train collision appears on these front pages. The *Southern Metropolis Daily*, in contrast, features a photo of the crashed trains and derailing cars taking up two-thirds of the front page, with a bold, large font headline that reads "High speed trains collide in Wenzhou; Four cars fall off bridge." The chief editor also projected Weibo posts demanding that those responsible for the accident be held to account. On one of the slides, the chief editor added his own assessment: "This kind of harsh questioning and serious attitude is the morality and conscience that Chinese citizens should have."

In term of range, the chief editor highlighted the breadth and volume of information posted on Weibo in the couple of days following the collision. He marveled that the sheer amount of information available on Weibo far surpassed that purveyed by regular news media. He pointed out that many of the photos taken on the scene and posted on Weibo, including pictures of the railway minister holding a press conference in an air-conditioned train car and the long line of volunteers waiting in the heat to donate blood, were absent from traditional media.

Lastly, the chief editor noted that Weibo discussion went considerably beyond the accident per se and turned into a much deeper assessment of a fundamental conflict in the Chinese society: the contradictions emerging from the government's aggressive pursuit of GDP growth while neglecting common people's well-being. The chief editor cited Tong Dahuan's Weibo post as an example of such depth.

After the presentation, the chief editor urged people at the meeting to pay more attention to Weibo, not just as a source of information but also as an inspiration to change their values about news. He also encouraged his colleagues to be braver in expressing their opinions, on Weibo as well as in the paper. "Try not to let Sina close your account," he said, referring to the mandatory monitoring the government expects from Internet service providers, "but at the same time take advantage of freedom of speech" (July 25).

The influence of Weibo on traditional media triggered by the train collision was no flash in the pan. It endured in the newsroom through the remainder of my fieldwork, and emerged constantly in newsroom meetings and conversations. More than a month later, for instance, on September 13, this chief editor again mentioned the train collision at an editorial meeting, in connection with his paper's coverage of a ferryboat sinking in Hunan. Nine middle school students and three adults had drowned in the boat accident, and the paper's story had raised questions about how and why it came about. Still, the chief editor thought the coverage was too timid, and suggested the role of government failings deserved harsher treatment and that his staff should have followed more closely "the train coverage approach" (September 13). The 7.23 train collision illustrates the powerful influence the Internet and new media can exert upon traditional journalism and journalists. Besides being a major source of information, Weibo conveyed priorities, attitudes, and values very different from those emphasized in mainstream state media, inspiring journalists at Kunming metro papers to likewise challenge conventions and test limits, as discussed in detail below from five aspects.

New Source of Information

Conversations with journalists and newsroom observations made it clear that Weibo has become a major source of story ideas for journalists. A reporter who covers police, court, and local government said consulting Weibo regularly is now a must, and that he browses through Weibo posts for 30 minutes at a time at least twice a day (August 8). An editor confessed to having some kind of Weibo anxiety syndrome, in that he feels compelled to check Weibo all the time for fear that he has missed something significant. And I could not help but notice a night editor's repetitive reference during a nighttime budget meeting: "on Weibo, it says . . ."; "on Weibo, I saw . . ." (August 17).

Here is one example of how Weibo provided a story idea. At about 3:00 p.m. one day, a web editor, who oversees the content of the website of a metro paper, excitedly announced breaking news—the release of a provincial government report on furniture purchases for the Yunnan Party Academy, a training institute for Party officials. The report, intended to show openness about government purchases, said the institute had spent more than 11 million yuan (about US$1.75 million) on furniture. Already, postings on Weibo were calling this lavish spending and suggesting such amounts could be better spent on other uses, such as sending poor children to school. A Weibo post about the matter by an editor from another local paper whom the web editor followed, and reposted by many others, had drawn the web editor's attention. He traced the information back to the government website where the report had appeared, and then alerted the reporters' department. He and a reporter then communicated through an instant messaging service on the computer about how to conduct interviews and produce stories for both the newspaper and the website (August 9).

Information concerning government conduct is well guarded in China, and until very recently Chinese government agencies did not hold news conferences, not to mention their habitual cover up of "bad news" as seen in the early stage of the outbreak of SARS in 2003 (Brady, 2008). The Internet and social media like Weibo, with millions of people, including government agencies themselves, posting tremendous amount of information every minute, certainly have provided additional channels of information flow, allowing journalists to discover stories that otherwise will not come to light.

Expanding the Range of Discourse

The Wenzhou train collision is a case in point of Weibo's power in broadening the scope of the conversation, as already mentioned. In a matter of a few days, the public discourse on Weibo went considerably beyond the accident per se to highlight a fundamental conflict between aggressive pursuit of GDP growth and public safety. But even before the train collision, journalists have realized the value of Internet discussion in broadening the range of public discourse. One metro paper in Kunming decided two years before to devote an entire page every day to stories that originated from the Internet, including BBS discussions and Weibo comments.

The purpose of a page like this, according to the page editor, is "to expand the range of speech." A regular news account about a government official's talk, for instance, will be straightforward. But if anything the official said offended the public, comments and criticism that people have posted online turn the story into an Internet event suitable for the web story page, said the editor. On any given day, the editor usually chooses topics, debates, or events that have generated the most comments or reposts on Weibo. This editor has come to see the Internet as the sole media channel enjoying some degree of freedom, where people can express, discuss, debate, or simply complain with fewer restrictions. "Traditional media [in China] are castrated, missing a lot of functions, which are supplemented by the Internet," he said, and the web story page is how his paper tries to recover some of the media's lost functions (October 26). "There are too many sensitive terms now," he said, and brought up a prominent Chinese artist critical of the Chinese government whose name media organizations are told not to use: "Why is Ai Weiwei a sensitive term? He is just an artist." In fact, the editor said, the paper sometimes had used sensitive terms in stories. "Why something is sensitive? At least tell me the reason. If no reason could be provided, why not go one step forward?" (September 28).

One day, for example, the editor spotted a heated discussion on Weibo, regarding rumors circulating online that a government cemetery for "revolutionary martyrs" had decided to relocate the tomb of a hero of China's Republican Revolution, led by the Kuomintang or Nationalist Party, which overthrew the Qing Dynasty, to make room for some Communist revolutionaries' tombs. On Weibo, many people expressed disgust at what they interpreted as officials' disrespecting history and instead trying to curry favor with higher authorities. He knew the issue was fraught with political sensitivity—essentially, it amounted to a Communist Party rivalry with its old enemy, the Kuomintang. But he did not want to succumb to what he saw as unnecessary taboos. He published the story.

In all, the editor uses the web story page, which relies heavily on social media for story ideas, to report on topics normally classified as sensitive, and affiliating his page with the Internet allows him more latitude versus editing a traditional newspaper page. Despite limitations imposed by the government, he has been able to push the boundaries and go beyond the scope of newspaper coverage normally allowed in China.

Defying Censorship

While print editors in general are still somewhat cautious about pressing limits, the editor at one newspaper's website is more audacious. He once invited an unconventional candidate for representative to the local People's Congress—an outspoken woman who had nominated herself—for a conversation, which was streamed live on Weibo and allowed real-time participation from the public. This was despite the fact that provincial propaganda authorities had explicitly banned media coverage of self-nominated grassroots candidate for legislature. The conversation started at 2:30 p.m., and at about 5 p.m. came a call from propaganda officials to the paper's deputy chief editor, requesting the event's termination. The web editor duly stopped the live chat. The deputy chief editor also said the related web story about the conversation that was at the top of the homepage needed to be demoted.

The web editor did not listen to that part. He waited in his office until 6 p.m., when he figured the bureaucrats had left work, and then he went home, leaving the homepage as it was until the next morning. He did delete two particularly sensitive comments from the web story but he kept the entire content on the newspaper's Weibo account, over which propaganda authorities had less control because, according to the editor, officials wishing to change material on Weibo would need to contact sina.com.cn, the commercial host (August 25). Other reporters have told me incidents where their story was killed for political or business reasons, and they turned the gist of the story into 140 characters to post on Weibo, somehow still getting the message out (October 12, III).

Pushing for More Government Transparency

Besides allowing some leeway around censorship, many journalists also believe that new communication technologies are compelling the government to become more transparent, a significant change given the Chinese government's reputation of withholding information from the media and public. For one thing, many government agencies and their media relations people have opened Weibo accounts, which are keenly followed by many journalists. These Weibo accounts open up communication channels that can produce better and quicker results than phoning, because Chinese government officials or spokesperson are usually hard to reach over the phone. The website editor mentioned above, for example, often posts or reposts rumors or news tips on Weibo and finds he sometimes can get a response from media relations personnel of the government by directing his postings to relevant Weibo accounts, using "@." The Weibo system will notify an account when someone else posts with an @.

A journalist who used to cover the police said the Internet and social media have made authorities realize that few happenings can be covered up, and some have learned to share information in a timely manner (September 22, I). Others agree: "Before, government officials could simply say, I just won't talk to you. Now because of the Internet, there are more monitoring channels and the government has to talk," said another reporter (October 21, I).

Many journalists agree that social media and the Internet are altering the media environment in significant ways. "The shackles will open, especially in the era of the Internet and self-media," said a newspaper executive. "The breakthrough for the media environment lies in the revolution of technology. The push from the bottom up could reach the goal of enabling the media to control their own coverage." And in these new circumstances, efforts to rein in media can even backfire. When local papers were banned from covering the new trend of citizens nominating themselves as candidates for political office, everyone could learn about it through Weibo. "Not allowing coverage actually puts pressure on the government," the executive said, because it only provides yet another case of the government trying to silence the media and people can take it to social media to condemn the suppression (October 12, I).

Viral Impact

The capacious reach of the Internet and the sharing ability of social media have made some journalists' work more influential than mere distribution of the print newspaper would suggest. A story about chemical pollution in a city not far from Kunming was a case in point. Large amounts of industrial waste containing cadmium, which is toxic when absorbed in water and soil, had been dumped on the grounds of a village instead of being transported to a designated site for proper disposal. Some of the waste was said to have been dumped in a river upstream from the Pearl River, which runs through

Guangdong and Guangxi Provinces. Paper B did a story on this matter and the story was posted on Weibo by some readers, who also speculated that the toxins would flow all the way to Guangdong and Guangxi, which are more populous and economically prominent than Yunnan. All of a sudden, the story became a huge hit and prompted the central government to send investigators. "This matter becoming so big should be credited to the power of the Internet," the journalist on the story said. In fact, he added, many of the Weibo posts circulated unconfirmed rumors, which he said he tried to correct with his own Weibo postings. Nonetheless, thanks to Weibo, the impact of the story greatly exceeded his expectations (October 8, II).

An executive from one paper said social media support the belief that "to watch is a power," a phrase referring to public attention and sharing on Weibo. Every time someone reposts or comments on a Weibo post, it generates more public attention that puts pressure on the authorities, thus a better chance for problems reported to be solved (September 18). Throughout the study, the journalists have expressed a lot of frustration over how little real impact their news coverage can have on social issues, be it official corruption, environmental pollution, or disparity between the rich and the poor. The root problem, as the journalists see it, is the lack of electoral right of the people and the one-party ruling system. Social media, now it seems, have empowered the common people and the journalists to make their voice heard and even move the needle to some extent, and the journalists are excited about it.

The abovementioned five aspects of social media impact are useful not just for this study, but can be applied to examine how social media can allow more freedom of the press in other societies with press control, where journalists are struggling to have more freedom.

Meanwhile, social media are not omnipotent, in China or elsewhere. It is necessary to note their limitations.

Constraints on the Power of Social Media

As some scholars have noted, the Internet in itself is neither liberating nor revolutionary (Shie, 2004). From the onset, the Chinese government was wary of digital technologies that might present new avenues to challenge state control but recognized that Internet development was essential to China's economic growth and global integration (Endeshaw, 2004). The Party thus has endeavored to use the benefits of the Internet to strengthen its power, while using controlling measures to keep political risks to a minimum (Tai, 2006; Zheng, 2007; Zhou, 2005). The Central Propaganda Department and State Council Information Office, for instance, are mainly concerned about squelching political discourse on the Internet and have issued or supported numerous regulations limiting political discussion online, applied blocking and filtering technologies, deployed cyber-cop monitors and, when challenged, police powers, including arrests of dissidents (Endeshaw, 2004; Lacharite, 2002; Shie, 2004; Tai, 2006; Zheng, 2007).

Various state regulations and constant watch from the authorities obstruct journalists' use of technology to its full potential. The web story page mentioned above, for example, operates under various constraints. Similar pages were appearing in papers across the country around the same time as in Kunming, and the propaganda authorities took notice. According to a metro paper executive, authorities tried to control the trend by requiring stories on such pages to be verified with offline sources before being published (September 18). This rule imposes additional work on reporters and editors of these pages, because they cannot simply relay and attribute Internet content. In addition, the web story page editor said he adhered to the "red line" when it was clear. "If news administrators say something better not to be covered, then we'd better not." But he will pursue situations allowing for leeway. "If it looks like propaganda authorities haven't said anything, then we can do it" (October 26).

Tabloids in Kunming also see their hands tied in multimedia production due to regulations that restrict posting of original videos to their own websites. One Kunming paper devotes great efforts to multimedia coverage but is not allowed to post original videos directly on its own website. It has to upload video to one of the authority-approved video hosting sites and then embed the video on its own website, which often causes delay or even failure in the posting (July 20). Knowing the constant frustration over uncertainty and delay, one photographer at the paper decided to post a video he produced, which depicts city patrol officers beating up a street vendor in front of the vendor's young child, on his own Weibo account rather than having to go through all the trouble to have it posted on his newspaper's website, which might well never happen (September 28). He chose unhampered and timely publication over a more legitimate sense of his work.

In addition, reporters' postings on social media may bring unwanted attention from the authorities. One evening when a reporter had just filed a story about a recent court case, his editor yelled from another side of the newsroom that the provincial Supreme Court had sent a message to kill the story because it had something to do with a controversial case. "Coverage of anything related to Li Changkui is not allowed," said the editor. "What kind of reason is this?" the reporter protested and insisted the case in his story had nothing to do with Li Changkui, a convicted rapist and murderer whose sentence to less than the death penalty had angered the public and created a public relations crisis for the provincial Supreme Court.

Moments later, an editor of a higher rank walked in the newsroom, and the reporter pleaded to him. The editor noted that the reporter had mentioned the case on Weibo and compared it with the Li Changkui case. "The Weibo post was just for fun," the reporter said. Evidently, however, the authorities did not see it as fun but took the association, made by the reporter himself, very seriously. After further discussion, editors decided that if the reporter could get people at the provincial Supreme Court to agree to publication, it could go ahead. The reporter was confident he could get court officials to sign off the story and planned to seek clearance the next day (October 12, II).

By and large, social media have inspired a new imagination among the journalists of a free press, all the while providing the actual tools that could be used to materialize that imagination, albeit to a limited extent. Social media also have become the new battleground where the journalists fight against press control and, despite the strong hand of the authorities, they have nonetheless offered the journalists some new hope for more changes to come. The political context in China, meanwhile, remains more or less the same. Facebook and Twitter are still not accessible and the government still closely monitors and controls social media (see more discussion on that in the Conclusion of this volume). With technology evolving fast but the political system trailing, the tension between journalists' pursuit of more press freedom and the restraining forces in China is more than likely to continue, hence the continuing aspiration and frustration. Social media, when allowing the reporter to say more and have a bigger impact, reconcile the frustration. The future is uncertain, but journalists in China will continue to seek change and social media may very well play an even bigger role.

Recent Developments

The research was conducted in 2011 and technology has been advancing quickly since then. Sina Weibo's dominance over social media has been challenged by a new comer, WeChat, or Weixin. Launched in 2011 as a mobile chatting service, WeChat has experienced substantial growth in the past five years to reach 650 million monthly active users by the end of 2015 (Millward, 2016). Weibo, in contrast, reached 212 million monthly active users by the second quarter of 2015 (Millward, 2015). WeChat does a better job than Weibo in facilitating communication among friends, whereas Weibo is a more open and public forum, allowing people to broadcast their opinions in the public domain rather than just within circles of friends as on WeChat. Due to its public nature, Weibo still possesses a unique position in journalism

WeChat, on the other hand, has no 140-character limit and essentially allow news organizations to build an entire news platform on it. The official website of China's top Party organ, *People's Daily*, for example, has a

WeChat account that people can choose to follow. Anybody who follows that account will see about a dozen full-length news articles, with videos and photos, every day. There are also quite a few digital native news outlets that provides content through WeChat, such as *The Paper*, or *Pengpai News* (Tatlow, 2016). Roughly speaking, Weibo functions more like Twitter, and WeChat, Facebook.

Whereas Weibo and WeChat have helped journalists to push the media coverage boundaries in one way or another, these social media platforms, especially WeChat, have posed serious challenges to the very survival of metro papers. As a matter of fact, one of the four metro papers I studied for this book ceased publication in July 2015 after continuous decrease in revenue and prolonged back pay to its staff. The paper was associated with the Yunnan Association for the Handicapped, a semi-official organization, but its finance and daily operation was controlled by a company based in Fujian, which decided to stop running the paper (Xiao, 2015). My sources in Kunming also told me that other metro papers there are struggling to stay alive for the same reason: More people are getting their information on their Internet-connected mobile phones, and the readership of print newspaper is in sharp decline.

The challenge for the Kunming newspaper industry is also facing the rest of the country. Based on data released by China Internet Network Information Center, mobile access to the Internet has increased steadily among Chinese Internet users in recent years. In 2007, only 24% of Internet users access the Internet through their mobile phones. That percentage jumped to 90% by the end of 2015, at more than 600 million people (CNNIC, 2016). Widespread use of smart phones and people's changing habit of accessing the Internet through their phones are taking away readership from the print media.

Based on a report by international consulting company Deloitte, in 2012, metro papers claimed about 72% of the newspaper market in China, but also in 2012, newspaper advertisement revenue saw its decrease for the first time in three decades. In the same year, income and profit of China's newspaper industry started to see negative growth. The Deloitte report therefore claims that due to the fast rise of Internet use, China's newspaper industry has entered a "harsh winter" (Hou et al., 2014, p. 4). The downward trend continued into 2014, when the newspaper industry's revenue decreased 10% compared with a year ago, and profits were down 12.8%, according to data provided by China's State Administration of Press, Publishing, Radio, Film and TV (Tian, 2014). The same trend was seen in local markets. In Zhejiang Province, for example, nine out of 10 local newspaper groups saw a decrease in ad revenue in the first few months of 2016, and metro papers were the ones that took the biggest hit (Yu, 2016).

In fact, in 2011, Kunming metro papers already saw this coming. One newspaper executive considered the transformation to digital media a life-or-death issue for his news organization. Before I arrived in 2011, his paper had purchased an iPhone4, the newest model at that time, for each of its 80 reporters and editors, who were told to "play with it" and obtain some experience of digital journalism. One day, the executive summoned a group of reporters and editors to a meeting to discuss the new media transformation, which he said, "is already imminent" and was a matter of survival. "If we don't change, two years from now many people will lose their jobs," he said (August 23). Not coincidently, this editor later left the newspaper to work for a digital company.

Amid such drastic transition, journalists at local metro papers might shift their priority from trying to make social change to just keeping their jobs alive. Meanwhile, new forms of journalism started to emerge on various digital platforms. Aspiration, frustration, and reconciliation will continue to exist, with a digital twist.

References

Bao, Z. (2011, August 1). 甬动 [Yong dong]. *Shenghuo Xinbao*, pp. 18.

Brady, A. (2008). *Marketing dictatorship: Propaganda and thought work in contemporary China*. Lanham, MD: Rowman & Littlefield.

CNNIC. (2016). *CNNIC 第37次中国互联网统计报告 [CNNIC 37th statistical report on Internet development in China]*. Retrieved on May 5, 2016 from http://tech.sina.com.cn/z/CNNIC37/

Endeshaw, A. (2004). Internet regulation in China: The never-ending cat and mouse game. *Information & Communications Technology Law, 13*(1), 41–57. doi: 10.1080/1360083042000190634

Hou, P., Li, S., Wu, T., & Cathy, L. (2014). *中国报业的危机与涅磐时刻 [The crisis and Nirvana moment of China's newspaper industry]*. Retrieved May 4, 2016, from http://www2.deloitte.com/cn/zh/pages/technology-media-and-telecommunications/articles/china-newspaper-industry-crisis-and-rebirth.html

Johnson, I. (2011, July 25). Train wreck in China heightens unease on safety standards. *New York Times*, p. A4.

Lacharite, J. (2002). Electronic decentralisation in China: A critical analysis of Internet filtering policies in the people's republic of China. *Australian Journal of Political Science, 37*(2), 333–346. doi: 10.1080/10361140220148188

Millward, S. (2015). *Weibo hits 212M monthly active users, most now on mobile*. Retrieved May 9, 2016, from https://www.techinasia.com/weibo-212-million-active-users

Millward, S. (2016). *WeChat is 5 years old. Here's how it's grown*. Retrieved May 6, 2016, from https://www.techinasia.com/5-years-of-wechat

Osnos, E. (2012). *Boss rail: The disaster that exposed the underside of the boom*. Retrieved October 24, 2012, from http://www.newyorker.com/reporting/2012/10/22/121022fa_fact_osnos?currentPag

Repnikova, M. (2014). Investigative journalists' coping tactics in a restrictive media environment. In M. Svensson, E. Saether & Z. Zhang (Eds.), *Chinese investigative journalists' dreams: Autonomy, agency and voice* (pp. 113–132). Lanham, MD: Lexington Books.

Shie, T. R. (2004). The tangled web: Does the Internet offer promise or peril for the Chinese communist party? *Journal of Contemporary China, 13*(40), 523–540. doi: 10.1080/1067056042000213328

Tai, Z. (2006). *The Internet in China: Cyberspace and civil society.* London: Routledge.

Tatlow, D. K. (2016, 4/6). New tone in Chinese media. *New York Times*, p. B1.

Tian, S. (2016, January 14). 成本倒挂时代,能否给报业降税 [In the age of cost higher than revenue, can the newspaper industry pay less tax]? *Jinan Times*, p. A1.

Tong, D. (2011). 中国, 请你慢些走 *[China, please walk a little more slowly]* Retrieved January 11, 2012, from http://tongdahuan.qzone.qq.com/

Wines, M., & LaFraniere, S. (2011, July 29). In baring facts of train crash, blogs erode China censorship. *New York Times*, p. A1.

Xiao, H. (2015). 生活新报7月1日起正式停刊, 记者编辑被欠数月工资 [*New Life Daily to stop publication on July 1; reporters and editors owed salary for months*]. Retrieved May 5, 2016, from http://news.sohu.com/20150702/n416044112.shtml

Xinhua Net. (2011). 网民微博曝出温州列车追尾事故早于媒体两小时 [*Netizens broke the news of Wenzhou train collision on Weibo two hours earlier the media*]. Retrieved July 26, 2011, from http://news.cnwest.com/content/2011–07/24/content_4930928.htm

Yu, S. (2016). 调查:转型中的地市报业现状 [*Investigation: Current situation of local newspaper industry amid transition*]. Retrieved May 4, 2016, from http://www.mediacircle.cn/?p=35617

Zheng, Y. (2007). *Technological empowerment: The Internet, state, and society in China.* Stanford, CA: Stanford University Press.

Zhou, Y. (2005). *Historicizing online politics: Telegraphy, the Internet, and political participation in China.* Stanford, CA: Stanford University Press.

9 Journalism Culture With Chinese Characteristics

Having discussed in detail various aspects of journalism culture in Kunming based on findings from my field research, this volume now turns to analyze the journalism culture in light of its specific position in time and place: contemporary China, a society undergoing profound social transition in an increasingly globalized world. Journalism culture in Kunming reflects and embodies the traits of its time and place. It is journalism culture "with Chinese characteristics," to use a common Chinese political phrase. Although this is a study mostly focusing on the occupational level of journalism, it is necessary to look below as well as beyond this level to contextualize the findings.

Organizational Differences

The previous chapters drew on findings from four metro papers I studied in Kunming, discussing occupational culture traits shared among journalists at all four. However, it needs to be noted that there are some subtle and nuanced differences among the different news organizations. In particular, although they all face constraints, their status and organizational characteristics give rise to some different perceptions of and reactions to these constraints. As Lin (2008) once pointed out, social control exhibits differing patterns in Party organ vs. market-oriented newspapers, indicating variations among different news organizations.

Paper A is funded and operated by a privately owned media company, and the semi-official organization with which it is affiliated for regulatory purposes serves only as nominal sponsor and supervisor, involved neither in the daily business of the paper nor in supporting the paper financially. As such, this paper has the weakest political backing among the four metro papers, which in turn sometimes affects news choices. For instance, editors decided not to run a follow-up on a chemical pollution story broken by a competing paper, despite obvious interest in the matter, because they felt they lacked the clout to defy a provincial propaganda ban on local media's further coverage of the topic. Unlike other papers affiliated with the municipal and provincial Party committees, the paper had no powerful political patrons to help fend off trouble if it stepped over the line. One editor compared the likely prospects to soccer: Angering the authorities would draw a "yellow card" warning for the first time, and after two yellow cards, the paper would be shut down, throwing hundreds of people out of work. For the same reason, other ideas also were out of the question, such as a story assessing the negative impact of Kunming's subway construction. "It is a municipal project and you want to criticize it? No!" the editor said (August 15).

On the other hand, simply being affiliated with Party organs and having closer ties with political power does not automatically lead to more daring news coverage. Sometimes the result is quite the opposite. News producers at papers C and D, which have stronger ties with the authorities, generally emphasize playing it safe and actually adhere more strictly to the boundaries. An executive at one of these papers said his priority is "news safety," making sure his paper will be alive and well. An executive at the other, originally created by and still affiliated with the province's top Party organ, admits to having inherited some official habits and conventions. The legacy is "both treasure and burden," he said, and then cited a common Chinese description of the press: "We are dancing while wearing shackles." Although his paper enjoys more circulation and influence than other local metro papers, it would pay a high price for making mistakes, the executive said. Other papers that run stories provincial authorities warn against might face a scolding, he said, whereas if his paper defies a warning, "the punishment will be harsher and more concrete."

Furthermore, as a publication under a large province-run news conglomerate, Paper C does not control its own human resources and finances and is answerable to its parent paper, the provincial Party organ, which can demand that certain stories run and other stories don't. The executive calls his metro paper "moderate conservative," saying it is relatively "obedient" and also loathes to damage "good relations" with government agencies and authorities. All these elements make covering sensitive issues and monitoring the authorities harder, and when the paper extends itself, care must be taken: "No hyping, no exaggerating headlines, no front page coverage, no full page, no multiple photos," the executive said. Trying to monitor public power is still essential, he said, but his staff must be moderate, and never too negative, and they intend to maintain this style (October 12, I).

In contrast, Paper B, whose editorial operations are controlled by a large media group based in Guangdong Province, is more audacious in its news coverage and display. This paper employs loud headlines and showy photos and does not shy away from putting sensitive stories on the front page or using full- and even multiple-page coverage. In fact, its parent company owns several regional publications with national reputations for boldness, which gives this Kunming metro paper both exemplars and fortitude for departing from conventions and taking risks (October 21, II). "Party papers serve the leaders, we serve the readers," said an executive at this metro, adding that his paper strives to demonstrate the same values of social justice and fairness upheld by its better-known cousins (September 21). Nonetheless, like everybody else, journalists at this paper still watch out for the red line that cannot be crossed.

Such organizational differences may influence journalists' professional ideals. Lin's (2010) survey indicated that journalists working for Party organs or market-oriented media outlets have different opinions regarding the news organization's watchdog role, the literati tradition, Western journalism, and advocacy. For example, it is more likely that a journalist who works for a Party organ will have a positive attitude toward the literati tradition than his colleagues in a market-oriented media organization. Also, a journalist who works in an organization with more circulation will have more positive views of Western professionalism than those in organizations with lower circulation. Such variations were not the focus of the current study, which paid more attention to shared characteristics, but can be further explored by future studies.

Kunming and China

The three aspects of the journalism culture found in Kunming, aspiration, frustration, and reconciliation, more or less resonate with studies on other groups of journalists in various locations in China. Earlier studies of Chinese news workers have focused on journalists working in prominent political and economic centers, chiefly Beijing and Shanghai, with some attention to the southern province of Guangdong. It is useful to learn that journalists in Kunming, capital city of a border province, share much of the ethos of their peers in better-studied places.

In terms of aspiration, what is found among Kunming journalists, such as concern for lower social strata and desire to monitor power, have long been documented in studies of Chinese journalists (Burgh, 2003; Polumbaum, 1990, 2008). Chinese journalists interviewed by Polumbaum (2008), for example, expressed similar aspirations to advance social justice and monitor the powerful. One of these journalists spent years covering the hardship of migrants displaced by the construction of the grand Three Gorges Dam; another exposed the Beijing municipal government's demolition of historic neighborhoods.

Such courage to defy the authorities and passion for political change were also exhibited among journalists in the 1980s, during the first decade of the post-Mao reforms, when many intellectuals believed China was ready for a different political system, with more democracy and freedom. These journalists included newspaper editor Qin Benli and his colleagues, who pressed for more political freedom up until their Shanghai paper, the *World Economic Herald*, was shut down in the period leading up to the June 4, 1989, crackdown on protesters (Hsiao & Yang, 1990). Reporters and editors at the Beijing-based *Science and Technology Daily* acted similarly and reported profusely on the student demonstrations in Tiananmen Square. At one point, hearing that the government might stop distribution to postal carriers, staff themselves carried stacks of papers to post offices around Beijing for delivery (Goldman, 1994). Like them, some of the journalists in Kunming expressed desires to see fundamental changes of the state system and aspired for a freer, fairer, and more democratic China.

Meanwhile, the sort of bedevilment by constraint, frustration, disappointment, and discontent that I found among journalists in Kunming is also common in much of the scholarly literature on Chinese journalism in the reform era (Donald & Keane, 2002; He, 2000; Pan, 2000; Pan & Lu, 2003; Polumbaum, 1990, 2008). In the immediate post–Cultural Revolution decade, up to the 1989 demonstrations, journalists in China wrestled with the challenges of "serving two masters," the Communist Party and the people, supposedly compatible missions that in reality could be at odds. Polumbaum (1990) described this as a tension between the interests of "hegemonic communication," furthering the ruling Party's ideological and political control, and "petitionary communication," representing the common people. In the early years of the reform era, Chinese journalists were shifting toward the latter mode even as circumstances often restricted them to the former.

With accelerated commercialization of media beginning in the 1990s, journalists increasingly found themselves now serving not two, but three masters: the Party, the people (in their role not merely as citizens but more and more as consumers), and advertisers (Donald & Keane, 2002). In addition to following the Party line, they now had to watch out for the bottom line as well (Zhao, 1998). At times, commercial interests and political demands pulled in opposite directions, and journalists found ever more creative methods to find a safe balance, as well as much cause for discontent with the circumstances of their work (He, 2000; Pan, 2000).

In one study, journalists participating in a survey ranked the importance of news media playing an independent watchdog function, or role-as-ideal, and their judgment of how well their current organizations perform this role, or role-in-practice. The survey revealed that the organizations' actual performance of the watchdog function falls short of the journalists' expectations (Lin, 2010). Such a discrepancy between role-as-ideal and role-in-practice corresponds with the discrepancy between journalists' aspiration and the reality they encounter described in the previous chapters of this volume. The current study further probed journalists' reaction to such a gap and revealed profound frustrations felt by these journalists.

Comparing with the pre-reform era, the boundaries on news coverage have expanded substantially. While crime news, critical news, and even human interest news were still sensitive areas of coverage in the 1980s (Polumbaum, 1990), they have become the mainstay of metro papers in Kunming. Yet, journalists in my study are still discontented, frustrated, and often disappointed, partly because now their expectations are even higher and they want greater political change, more press freedom, better protection of basic human rights, and a fairer society. Meanwhile they see problems remain, if not worse, from environmental pollution to social and economic disparities to official malfeasance and corruption (Buckley, 2012). Comparing my fieldwork findings to prior studies, I cannot help speculating that the agony of journalists in Kunming is even more severe than the tribulations of preceding generations of Chinese journalists.

One way to combat such frustration is finding ways of reconciliation or compromise. Besides what is discussed about the Kunming journalists, other studies have observed various ways of Chinese journalists trying to go around constraints and achieve something. For example, one tactic that some investigative journalists use is waiting out sensitivity, delaying the publication of certain stories to avoid confronting the authorities head-on, but still making the story public. Investigative journalists also use other negotiating strategies, like trying to be balanced in their reporting to avoid political fallout, accommodating official's interests by withholding certain information in exchange for publishing a story, and cross-regional coverage—revealing wrongdoings of officials in other places than their own local government, which has direct control of their publication (Repnikova, 2014). These negotiating strategies are similar to the compromises or reconciliations that this volume has discussed and also used by some of the Kunming journalists.

After all, Kunming is part of China, having more or less the same pulse as the rest of the country. The overarching transformation of Chinese media from being a Party mouthpiece to partly mouthpiece, partly political public relations agency, and partly business also determines the configuration of the newspaper industry in Kunming. At the national level, the constraints of political control combined with business pressures, the ambiguities and contradictions of a developing market economy under an authoritarian political system, and the tensions between continuity and change (Lee, 1994; Zhao, 1998) have, if anything, intensified by the time of the current study. Consequently, as elsewhere in China, journalists in Kunming are partly propaganda soldier, partly crusader and watchdog, partly just frustrated news worker. Such a multifaceted professional role, determined by the complex broader context, is a distinct Chinese characteristic.

While resonating with many of the previous studies, this volume does not just repeat the existing findings but endeavors to arrive at a holistic understanding of the occupational culture of metro paper journalists in Kunming through systemically examining their aspirations, frustrations, and reconciliations. In contrast with previous studies, this volume also presents several rather unique perspectives.

Investigative Journalists vs. Metro Paper Journalists

Prominent in previous studies on Chinese journalists is the subject of investigative journalists (e.g., Bandurski & Hala, 2010; Repnikova, 2014; Svensson et al., 2014; Tong, 2011), who are the elite and resonate well with Western journalism values. This study moves the gaze down the pyramid to focus on the grassroots of the journalist force, the typical day-to-day news workers in China, as already discussed in Chapter 1 of this volume. Nevertheless, metro paper journalists in Kunming share similar aspirations, frustrations, and reconciliations as China's investigative journalists—the desire to make a difference and to change the society for the better, the obstacles to reaching the goal, the tactics of bypassing the obstacles, such as undercover reporting, and the use of technology in pushing the boundaries (Bandurski & Hala, 2010; Svensson et al., 2014). What this study contributes is to ask, What does this all mean? How does this shape the occupational culture?

Literati vs. Citizens

In the previous studies, Chinese journalists are often classified as part of China's literati. They are deemed as heirs to the upright moral official of traditional China, who devoted power and prestige to improving people's livelihoods. Journalists of the Mao era saw themselves as both servant and savant, as bearer of culture for the nation, with responsibility to educate the ignorant masses (Cheek, 1997). They were not unlike traditional Confucian scholar-bureaucrats, caring about the common folks but from a top-down, paternalistic perspective. Highly literate and educated, they were part of the intelligentsia, belonging to social elites (Polumbaum, 1990). Such elitism continued into the post-Mao period as Deng Xiaoping launched the reforms. Reformist journalists at that time, such as the then *People's Daily* chief editor Hu Jiwei, sustained the tradition of the moral official trying to do good for the people (Polumbaum, 2002). Even during the reform era, the literati tradition is still seen as influential among journalists (Hassid, 2011; Lin, 2010).

On the other hand, Chinese journalists today could be said to have a fragmented sense of collective identity. Those working for top Party organs such as *People's Daily* still are defined as propaganda cadre and viewed as elite, and some working for publications targeting the well-educated or business elites pride themselves on being respectable professionals (Liu, 2000; Pan & Lu, 2003). But at the level of the metro papers, a new kind of differentiation is emerging.

Kunming journalists' analogy comparing their jobs to migrant labor marks a significant departure from the literati-associated group identity. The notion that journalists are migrant workers of words reflects a general decline in their occupational status over the past few decades. Since embarking on the path of truly dramatic marketization and much more active integration into the global economic system, the rapid commercialization of media has steadily eroded journalists' elite social standing. The rise of metro papers in particular nurtured a cohort who saw themselves less as elite intellectuals and more like service providers trying to please consumers (Liu, 2000; Sun, 2002). The growth of consumer culture also attenuated the belief that common people need moral officials or caring intellectuals to speak for them. Nowadays, they are consumers with consumer sovereignty (Donald & Keane, 2002), and media must care about what their audiences want in order to sell and make profits.

Journalists in Kunming gave no impression of subscribing to elitism. To the contrary, their migrant worker analogy—even if hyperbolic—puts them at the lowest tier of China's urban society. Although these journalists realize their work offers them a public platform and therefore carries some special powers and responsibilities, they don't hold a haughty view of themselves. Certainly it is unthinkable in Kunming's metro papers to hear anybody self-identify as a government functionary (*xuanchuan ganbu* or "propaganda cadre"), or even as an intellectual. These journalists are seen, and they see themselves, as aligned with the grassroots.

Therefore, their concern for the society is more from a citizen's perspective than that of social elites. They are no longer the educated few trying to figure out from top down the best way of life for the general public, but conscious citizens who are striving for a better society for themselves and their families from bottom up. This distinction is significant, because it is a result of decades of market-oriented reform, efforts to drive the media from the altar to the market, from an elite voice to popular consumption. Together with advance in general education and information technology, the status change of the journalists, some of them, at least, marks a significant step forward in the Chinese society: Finally, common people are worthy enough to be able to actually worry about the country and society and even do something about it, rather than having to rely on the educated elites to do that for them.

Professionalism vs. Journalism Culture

Party journalism has provided the framework for examining Chinese journalism for several decades (e.g., Zhao, 1998), until its decline in the 1990s as a result of the market-driven press reform. The old Party journalism model has started to phase out, but the new model has yet to find its footing (Lin, 2010). In academic studies, replacing the Party journalism framework seems to be the professionalism framework, as professionalism or professionalization became the buzz word among literature on Chinese journalism (e.g., Bai, 2012; Hassid, 2011; Lin, 2010; Pan & Lu, 2003). The current study, however, argues that the new analytical framework replacing Party journalism is not quite Western-style professionalism, but a distinct occupational culture with Chinese characteristics, because it allows a holistic examination of both ideas and practices of the journalists, situated in the specific context of China, and is more likely to reveal who these journalists really are.

Besides the reasons already presented in Chapter 1 of this volume, I avoided using professionalism as an analytic framework to study these journalists, because the essence of Western-style professionalism is to enable journalists to tell objective truth, which is precisely what Chinese journalists cannot do. They cannot remain objective, because there is simply too much social injustice (see Chapter 7 of this volume), driving them to side with the disadvantaged. They have even less capacity to tell the truth because there are various forces in China preventing them from revealing truth. To repeat the words of a veteran journalist: "Truth is in short supply in China" (quoted in Chapter 4 of this volume). My fieldwork made me realize that professionalism as practiced in the U.S. is almost a luxury for the metro paper journalists. There are many circumstances that would not allow them to be professional: They cannot use people's full names, they sometime conceal their identity as a reporter, they cannot always be fair and square, and above all, they are restrained from telling the truth. And yet, they still have a distinct occupational culture with Chinese characteristics.

Therefore, a better way to understand these journalists is to see them for who they are, assess the actual, concrete conditions under which they conduct their work, and understand, from their own perspective, what it means for them to do what they do. That is why the framework of journalism culture is a more effective way of understanding these journalists.

The Theoretical Framework

What, then, does the journalism culture framework actually entail? It needs to be noted that the term journalism culture is not an invention of the current study. Hanitzsch (2007), for example, has studied journalism culture at a global level. In his construct, journalism culture is articulated at three levels, cognitive, evaluative, and performative, with the first two concerning work definitions, worldviews, and occupational ideology and the last one tapping practices that materialize what has been shown at the first two levels. "Journalistic practices are shaped by cognitive and evaluative structures, and journalists—mostly unconsciously—perpetuate these deep structures through professional performance" (Hanitzsch, 2007, p. 369). A one-on-one correspondence between materialization and values is assumed in Hanitzsch's model.

The current study, in contrast, examines journalism culture at the local level, and the biggest difference between my findings and Hanitzsch's model is the discrepancy between the values expressed by the journalists (cognitive and evaluative) and their actual practice (performative). Another existing theoretical framework that I had attempted to use to explain my findings is the substance–form construct of occupational culture. This construct postulates two major dimensions of occupational culture: networks of meanings contained in sets of shared, sometimes taken-for-granted beliefs and values, or the *substance* of the culture, and mechanisms for expressing and affirming these beliefs, or cultural *forms*, including practices, behavior, rituals, and rites (Trice, 1993; Trice & Beyer, 1984). But again, such a construct assumes a correspondence between the substance and form of a particular occupational culture.

In my study, however, it is observed that some values are expressed but not practiced, and some practices do not necessarily match the expressed values. In the particular journalism culture explored here, there is clearly a gap between what the journalists aspire to do and what they actually can accomplish, between their definitions and conceptions of their work and actual practice. In other words, under specific social conditions, journalists' ideas and practices do not automatically and seamlessly correspond with each other. Journalists themselves, at the same time, are well aware of the gap between ideals and reality. This is primarily what produces their profound and prevalent sense of frustration, disappointment, and discontent.

Therefore, to fully understand a journalism culture, it is not adequate to just sort out the substance and form, or the ideas and practices, of a certain group of journalists. Rather, it is crucial and frankly, more fruitful, to look beyond what journalists think and do as well as how these two aspects resonate with each other and pay attention to the gaps and discrepancies between the ideas and practices. These gaps and discrepancies, in turn, may tell more about both the journalism culture and the broader enveloping culture and lead to a more comprehensive, deeper, and nuanced understanding of that particular journalism culture.

When existing theoretical frameworks cannot adequately explain the data I gathered in the field, I resorted to the grounded theory approach to find my own theoretical framework. The grounded theory approach strives to discover theories through systematic analysis of data, providing modes of conceptualization for describing and explaining what is found in the field. A grounded theory, derived from data, shall fit or work in a substantive, or empirical, area of inquiry, such as the occupational culture of journalism. The goal is not to provide a grand theory that explains the whole field through random sampling, but to generate conceptual categories and their conceptual properties that provide a different perspective of explaining particular behaviors and answering particular questions (Glaser & Strauss, 1967). In my study, conceptual categories and their properties were generated from the field study data to provide a new perspective of explaining how journalists in Kunming's metro papers giving meaning to their work and form their unique occupational culture. The categories I generated from the data are aspiration, frustration, and reconciliation, because together, they accommodate and explain most of my data and allow me to answer my research question: How do metro paper journalists in Kunming give meaning to their work? Geertz (1973) holds that culture is a web of meaning. The question of meaning is essentially a question of culture and therefore this study is a cultural inquiry.

Meanwhile, journalists do not operate in a vacuum and have to interact with the social surroundings. And therefore, from a sociological point of view, to make sense of how these journalists make sense of their work, the current study looks beyond the occupational setting and investigates how factors from the broader social settings (i.e., social conflict, political pressure, global influence, use of technology, etc.) influence different aspects of the occupational culture. In the realm of sociological inquiry of journalism, many studies have explored the process of news production, examining how individual characteristics, organizational routines, professional norms, media institution characteristics, social system, and cultural context help determine what gets into the news media (Berkowitz, 1997; Shoemaker & Reese, 1996; Shoemaker & Vos, 2009). Sociological study may reveal interactional determinants such as pattern of social interactions, relations and structures, whereas cultural study examines symbolic determinants such as values, beliefs, attitudes, and assumptions (Schudson, 1997/1989).

This volume, essentially, builds a bridge between these two modes of inquiry (i.e., cultural and sociological) through exploring the uniqueness of an occupational culture and its interrelations with the broader context. It tries to make the point that each journalism culture is different, with its unique characteristics related to some unique features of its residing society. In other words, this study tries to reach the end of a cultural inquiry (the meaning of being a metro paper journalist in today's China) through the means of sociological investigation (social factors that influence the meaning).

The theoretical framework, including its conceptual categories and their properties (in parenthesis), emerging from this study can be illustrated as following:

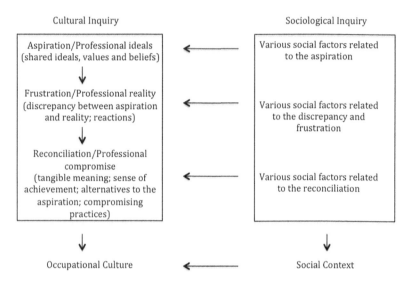

Figure 9.1 The Aspiration-Frustration-Reconciliation Framework

Based on this theoretical framework, a particular group of journalists can have their particular aspirations for their occupation, or their professional ideals (i.e., what they hope to achieve as journalists; what they aspire the meaning of being a journalist should be). Such aspirations are not always in sync with the reality, and the journalists face a discrepancy between what they aspire to achieve and what they can actually accomplish, due to various constraints influenced by elements in a given social environment: organizational, institutional, social, political, financial, and so on. The less-than-ideal professional reality may leave journalists frustrated to various degrees. But to make sense of their job and keep doing what they do, the journalists resort to certain kind of reconciliation, or professional compromise, something in between what they aspire and what they can actually materialize, between the ideal and the reality, which provides tangible meaning to their work. The three aspects together configure the occupational culture of a particular group of journalists. The actual aspiration, frustration, and reconciliation of journalists vary from society to society, culture to culture, even institution to institution. What kind of aspiration, frustration, and reconciliation the journalists hold reflect the distinct type of news organization, political system, society, and culture within which the journalists find themselves working.

The aspiration-frustration-reconciliation (or ideal-reality-compromise) construct provides a conceptual framework for understanding journalists' occupational culture from their own perspective, and allows more nuanced and in-depth assessment of the relationship between journalism and its specific social habitat. These categories, their properties and interrelations can also be quantified and measured, providing opportunities for further theoretical development.

As such, the theoretical contribution of this study does not lie in the testing or verifying of an existing theory or model, but the discovery of a theoretical framework that is grounded in the field research. Such discovery of grounded theory is important in sociological study because it encourages scholars to discover theories that can explain the tentative and specific situation in the field, as well as diverse and ever-changing social and human phenomena (Glaser & Strauss, 1967).

Some readers may question the similarity between this model and the theory of cognitive dissonance (Festinger, 1957). Indeed, the discrepancy between the journalist's professional ideal and reality can lead to frustration, or dissonance, and then there is this natural pressure to reduce such dissonance, leading to reconciliations or compromise. It is fair to say that Festinger's (1957) theory of cognitive dissonance does provide some psychological explanation of the sentiment and behavior of the journalists in my study. But there are several important differences between the aspiration-frustration-reconciliation framework and the theory of cognitive dissonance.

First, cognitive dissonance is "undoubtedly an everyday condition" (Festinger, 1957, p. 5) and can result from all kinds of daily behavior, but aspiration is a very special type of cognition; it is something one values and strives for. Not everybody has the kind of journalistic aspiration or ideal and the kind of frustration felt by the journalists, which is not exactly the same as everyday cognitive dissonance. It is a result of specific occupational, social, and political conditions and therefore has broader social and cultural implications.

Second, the current study deals with more work-related behavior than just personal behavior or behavior in general and therefore is more specific. Third, the theoretical framework presented in this volume and cognitive dissonance belong to two different realms, one is cultural inquiry of journalism and the other, social psychology. They answer two different sets of questions: one is how journalists give meaning to their work, and the other is how psychological consistency is achieved within an individual.

The feelings and behaviors of the journalists observed in this volume may well be explained from a social psychological point of view, using the theory of cognitive dissonance. However, instead of psychology, the purpose of this volume is to provide a framework that can help one understand the occupational culture of a particular group of journalists: how they give meaning to their work. It is also fairly common that the same group of people or social phenomenon can be examined from different perspectives, which supplement, rather than diminish, one another. Even if the aspiration-frustration-reconciliation model is not new in terms of social psychology, it is novel for exploring journalists' occupational culture, through examining the discrepancy between journalists' expectations and the reality of their profession, as well as, facing such incongruity, how they still find meaning in being a journalist.

References

Bai, H. (2012). 从倡导到中立：当代中国调查记者的职业角色变迁 [From initiative to neutrality: Changes in the professional roles of investigative journalists in contemporary China]. 新闻记者*[Journalism Review]*, 2.

Bandurski, D., & Hala, M. (Eds.) (2010). *Investigative journalism in China: Eight cases in Chinese watchdog journalism*. Hong Kong: Hong Kong University Press.

Berkowitz, D. (1997). Overview: Why a 'Social meaning of news' perspective? In D. Berkowitz (Ed.), *Social meaning of news* (pp. xi–xiv). Thousand Oaks, CA: Sage.

Buckley, C. (2012). *Exclusive: China president-in-waiting signals quicker reform—sources*. Retrieved September 7, 2012, from http://news.yahoo.com/exclusive-china-president-waiting-signals-quicker-reform-sources-075721240—business.html

Burgh, H. D. (2003). *The Chinese journalist: Mediating information in the world's most populous country*. London, New York: RoutledgeCurzon.

Cheek, T. (1997). *Propaganda and culture in Mao's China: Deng Tuo and the intelligentsia*. Broadbridge, UK: Clarendon Press.

Donald, S. H., & Keane, M. (2002). Media in China: New convergences, new approaches. In S. H. Donald, M. Keane & Y. Hong (Eds.), *Media in China: Consumption, content and crisis* (pp. 3–17). London: RoutledgeCurzon.

Festinger, L. (1957). *A theory of cognitive dissonance*. Stanford, CA: Stanford University Press.

Geertz, C. (1973). *The interpretation of cultures: Selected essays*. New York: Basic Books.

Glaser, B. G., & Strauss, A. L. (1967). *The discovery of grounded theory: Strategies for qualitative research*. New York: A. de Gruyter.

Goldman, M. (1994). The role of the press in post-Mao political struggles. In C. Lee (Ed.), *China's media, media's China* (pp. 23–36). Boulder, CO: Westview Press.

Hanitzsch, T. (2007). Deconstructing journalism culture: Toward a universal theory. *Communication Theory, 17*(4), 367–385. doi: 10.1111/j.1468–2885.2007.00303.x

Hassid, J. (2011). Four models of the fourth estate: A typology of contemporary Chinese journalists. *China Quarterly, 208*, 813–832.

He, Z. (2000). Chinese communist party press in a tug-of-war: A political-economy analysis of the *Shenzhen Special Zone Daily*. In C. Lee (Ed.), *Power, money, and media: Communication patterns and bureaucratic control in cultural China* (pp. 112–151). Evanston, IL: Northwestern University Press.

Hsiao, C., & Yang, M. (1990). "Don't force us to lie": The case of the *World Economic Herald*. In C. Lee (Ed.), *Voices of China: The interplay of politics and journalism* (pp. 111–121). New York: Guilford Press.

Lee, C. (1994). *China's media, media's China*. Boulder, CO: Westview Press.

Lin, F. (2008). *Turning gray: Transition of political communication in China 1978–2008*. Dissertation. University of Chicago, Chicago. Department of Sociology.

Lin, F. (2010). Organizational construction or individual's deed? The literati tradition in the journalistic professionalization in China. *International Journal of Communication, 4*, 175–197.

Liu, Y. (2000). 媒体中国 [*Media in China*]. Chengdu: Sichuan ren min chu ban she.

Pan, Z. (2000). Improving reform activities: The changing reality of journalistic practice in China. In C. Lee (Ed.), *Power, money, and media: Communication patterns and bureaucratic control in cultural China* (pp. 68–111). Evanston, IL: Northwestern University Press.

Pan, Z., & Lu, Y. (2003). Localizing professionalism: Discursive practices in China's media reforms. In C. Lee (Ed.), *Chinese media, global contexts* (pp. 215–236). London: Routledge.

Polumbaum, J. (1990). The tribulations of China's journalists after a decade of reform. In C. Lee (Ed.), *Voices of China: The interplay of politics and journalism* (pp. 33–68). New York: Guilford Press.

Polumbaum, J. (2002). Personality, biography and history: How Hu Jiwei strayed from the party path on the road to good citizenship. In M. Goldman & E. J. Perry (Eds.), *Changing meaning of citizenship in modern China* (pp. 187–211). Cambridge, MA: Harvard University Press.

Polumbaum, J. (2008). *China ink: The changing face of Chinese journalism*. Lanham, MD: Rowman & Littlefield.

Repnikova, M. (2014). Investigative journalists' coping tactics in a restrictive media environment. In M. Svensson, E. Saether & Z. Zhang (Eds.), *Chinese investigative journalists' dreams: Autonomy, agency and voice* (pp. 113–132). Lanham, MD: Lexington Books.

Schudson, M. (1997/1989). The sociology of news production. In D. Berkowitz (Ed.), *Social meaning of news* (pp. 7–22). Thousand Oaks, CA: Sage.

Shoemaker, P. J., & Reese, S. D. (1996). *Mediating the message: Theories of influences on mass media content*. White Plains, NY: Longman.

Shoemaker, P. J., & Vos, T. P. (2009). *Gatekeeping theory*. London, New York: Routledge.

Sun, Y. (2002). 报业中国 [*Newspaper industry in China*]. Beijing: Zhongguo san xia chu ban she.

Svensson, M., Saether, E., & Zhang, Z. (Eds.) (2014). *Chinese investigative journalists' dreams: Autonomy, agency and voice*. Lanham, MD: Lexington Books.

Tong, J. (2011). *Investigative journalism in China: Journalism, power, and society*. London: Continuum.

Trice, H. (1993). *Occupational subcultures in the workplace*. Ithaca, NY: ILR Press.
Trice, H. M., & Beyer, J. M. (1984). Studying organizational cultures through rites and ceremonials. *Academy of Management Review, 9*(4), 653.
Zhao, Y. (1998). *Media, market, and democracy in China: Between the party line and the bottom line*. Urbana, IL: University of Illinois Press.

Conclusion
Lessons Learned on Studying Journalism Culture

Through fieldwork of more than three months, the current study aims at exploring the journalism culture in a southwestern China metropolis, Kunming, answering the question of what and how journalists there give meaning to their work. This chapter summarizes the findings and theoretical contributions, while pointing to some directions for future studies.

Journalism Culture at Kunming Metro Papers

Participant observation, interviews, and analysis revealed a noticeable discrepancy between some of the meanings expressed by journalists and their actual practices, which cannot be fully explained by existing theoretical frameworks on occupational culture or journalism culture. In order to fully make sense of the data, a grounded theory approach was applied to analyze and sort through the data to arrive at three new categories: aspiration, frustration, and reconciliation. The main theoretical contribution of this volume lies in the formation of a new theoretical framework of studying a particular journalism culture, namely the aspiration-frustration-reconciliation (or ideal-reality-compromise) framework.

Using this new theoretical framework, this study provides an understanding of the journalism culture of metro newspaper journalists in Kunming. These journalists believe the meaning of their work lies in their ability to make a difference through their news coverage, such as pushing for political change toward greater political freedom and more accountable government, as well as making the society fairer and people's basic rights better protected. It is also meaningful for them to be the watchdog for the public through monitoring the powerful, revealing wrongdoings by government officials, authorities, powerful social institutions, and businesses, and having those responsible punished. These are their aspirations, their shared values, ideals, and beliefs.

In reality, however, political control from municipal, provincial, and central authorities, interference from authorities and nonauthorities alike to their reporting activities, frequent bans on various stories, the ultimate limit of the red line (issues concerning the one-party political system, conflicts between Han and ethnic minority groups, fundamental human rights, etc.), as well as pressure from advertisers, are obstructing the realization of their aspirations. Caught in between their aspiration and the dire reality, they express strong frustration and discontent, describing themselves as "conflicted." These sentiments constitute a distinct aspect of the meaning they assign to their work, indicated by their own perceived collective identity as "migrant worker of words/news." Such a collective identity reflects these journalists' contract-based employment as opposed to long-term hires as with the Leninist press system decades ago, their rather low social status as opposed to elite propaganda cadres in the past, as well as their mere income that can barely let them survive or afford the middle-class life.

In the midst of profound frustration, the journalists found more tangible ways to make their job meaningful and learned to compromise and reconcile, mostly through helping those in need, particularly the deprived, disadvantaged social strata in China. When sweeping, broad social changes are not attainable, the journalists resort to making smaller differences to gain a sense of achievement. They also try their best to monitor public power, although they have to mind the degree, learn not to make definitions, and often find themselves "beating up the fly instead of the tiger," or "monitoring only a drop of water instead of the whole body of the water," while maintaining the delicate enemy–friend relationship with the authorities. In addition, to carry out their perceived mission of being the watchdog, they often have to go undercover in order to reveal wrongdoings that harm public interests. In short, they have to compromise.

The study also found that the journalists bond with each other as a community through other cultural forms in their daily life in the newsroom. They get together for lunch and dinner, for weddings and New Year celebrations. They show off their voice at karaoke clubs or get drunk in bars. They share their stories, feelings, and opinions during these gatherings, as well as vices like chain-smoking. They are colleagues at work and friends off work. They poke fun at each other, tease each other, but also support each other. They laugh together, curse together, and fight for their dreams together.

Although this is a study mostly focusing on the occupational level of journalism, a better understanding of the occupation requires examining it in relation to elements below as well as beyond this level. At the organizational level, different news organizations have different perceptions and reactions to the constraints they face, some more obedient, some more defiant.

The current study also demonstrates how journalists' work intertwines with its social environment. As a result of China's aggressive seeking integration into the global system in recent decades, more and more Western values and ideas are presented to Chinese people. As shown in this volume, journalists in Kunming constantly use the West, especially the U.S., as a comparison framework, a prototype against which situation in China is evaluated, even though some of their ideas about the West are myths. Ideas and concepts from American journalism, such as objectivity, the Fourth Estate, and watchdog journalism, are appropriated by the journalists as an alternative symbolic resource to construct and express alternative values and ideals, or aspirations of their work.

Domestically, three pairs of social relations, between journalists and the authorities, the authorities and the disadvantaged, and the disadvantaged and journalists, greatly influence the way journalists give meaning to their work. Frequent conflicts between the disadvantaged and institutions, such as companies with government ties and state-run hospitals, usually subject the poor and powerless to a violation of their rights by the powerful, arousing journalists' desire to promote social justice and causing journalists to side with the disadvantaged. Rampant mistrust across the three pairs of social relations becomes the reason for journalists' attempt to monitor the authorities and authority obstruction to reporting in some cases, and adds to the already staggering frustration and disappointment among journalists when the very people they try to help abuse their sympathy and good will. At the same time, these social conditions compel the journalists to compromise, but also allow the journalists to find alternative ways of giving meaning to their work, such as helping those in need.

Another important aspect of the social environment is technology and social media, which have helped journalists in Kunming to push the boundaries of press freedom through providing new sources of information and more channels to discover stories ideas, broadening the range of public discourse to include topics eschewed by conventional media, allowing additional channels for news dissemination and therefore enabling journalists to defy censorship with the potential to go viral and generate bigger impact, and presenting more opportunities for journalists to interact with government officials and force the government to be more transparent to some degree.

It could be concluded that the journalism culture found in Kunming is one of testing limits and pushing boundaries, and of wide and deep frustration, given China's peculiar press system, which in some respects is set free to explore the market whereas in other ways is pulled back by an authoritarian government. The frustration is not despair, but a strong impulse for change, in accord with the Chinese society at large. The journalism culture is one of active involvement of local life, especially helping the poor and powerless, driven by deepening disparities among social strata and rising social conflicts in recent years. The journalism culture is one of appropriating Western ideas and practices, as well as new technologies, to help envision a country and a profession deemed better. The journalism culture is also one of contradictions and uncertainties, still in the making and changing at a rapid pace, just like China as a whole. It is a journalism culture of this particular era and place, in the midst of a profound social transformation, with Chinese characteristics.

Although studies on Chinese journalism from journalists' perspective are not in short supply (e.g., Burgh, 2003; Cheek, 1997; He, 2000, 2003; Hsiao & Yang, 1990; Pan, 2000; Pan & Lu, 2003; Polumbaum, 1990, 2008) and findings from the current study concur with many of the findings in previous studies, this study distinguishes itself in several ways. First, it devises a new theoretical framework of studying journalism culture, a theoretical framework that can be used in journalist groups other than metro newspapers and societies other than China. The aspiration-frustration-reconciliation framework allows holistic and systematic examination of both the ideals and practices, and the gap between them, of certain groups of journalists, situated within a certain social environment, to answer the question of what and how journalists give meaning to their work. Previous works also touched upon journalists' perception of the meaning of their work, but rarely invoked systematic cultural inquiry. The current study, therefore, contributes a new analytical framework to the scholarship of Chinese journalism and journalism studies in general.

Second, the current study addresses some of the newest trends in the ever-changing world of journalism in China, including the influence of social media and the development of a civil society. Although quite a few studies already address these recent changes, examining them from the perspective of the meaning of journalists' work is a rather novel approach.

Third, the current study is conducted in a place that has rarely been noticed by U.S.-based journalism scholars and focuses on a group of journalists, namely metro newspaper journalists, who have not gain sufficient academic attention. A study of journalism culture of metro paper journalists in Kunming expands the range of the literature through exploring a different locale than the often-studied places like Beijing or Shanghai and a different group of journalists, thus providing new knowledge on Chinese journalism.

Lessons Learned

Several lessons learned in the process of fieldwork and analysis are worth noting. First, the current study suggests that to fully understand a journalism culture, it is not adequate to just sort out the substance and form, or the ideals and practices, of a certain group of journalists. Rather, it is more fruitful to look beyond what journalists think and do, as well as how these two aspects resonate with each other, and pay attention to the gaps and discrepancies between the ideals and practices, which may well tell more about the journalism culture and the broader culture surrounding it.

Second, any journalism culture, including that in Kunming, is likely to be fluid rather than stable, especially in a rapidly changing context such as contemporary China. Journalists' views and ideas will be in flux as the society keeps transforming itself. Thus, an important lesson of my fieldwork is that in trying to understand a transitional society like today's China, one cannot expect a relatively well-formed, mature culture waiting to be analyzed, and the researcher needs to open his/her mind to fluidity, uncertainty, and contradictions, and indeed, embrace the noise and messiness as part of the culture. In Chinese society and culture at large, values, ideas, and behaviors are emerging, mixing, and disappearing all the time (Lynch, 1999; Zha, 1995).

Third, in China and elsewhere, journalism culture is no doubt an integral part of the broader culture, deeply intertwined with political, economic, cultural, social, and technological conditions surrounding it. News work may be analyzed as an occupational culture, but cannot be fully accounted for at the occupational level alone. Meaningful interpretation must involve higher levels of analysis, from institutional to national and even global (Berkowitz, 2011; Gans, 1979; Reese, 2001; Schudson, 1997[1989]; Shoemaker & Vos, 2009).

Last but not least, as a research project focusing on the perspective of journalists, the current study furthers a growing body of work debunking stereotypes of Chinese journalists (Burgh, 2003; Polumbaum, 2008). Far from being fearful, timid, and content acting as official mouthpiece, Chinese journalists are thoughtful and reflective, and many are courageous and full of passion and ideals. They are also able to accomplish a lot more than many people in the West might have imagined, as manifested in many major news events such as the 2008 Sichuan earthquake (Larson, 2011). They face the challenge of producing high-quality and meaningful journalism under state control and within a propaganda framework and are constantly testing the parameters. As Polumbaum (2008) puts it, for the best of China's journalists, "the adventure of making sense of dynamic and bewildering times is a mission, privilege and honor, and its own reward" (p. 9). They might feel frustrated and conflicted, yet many continue to fight for what they believe and aspire to achieve.

In all, journalists in China constantly seek their professional identity and occupational meaning in the intricacy of aspiration, frustration, and reconciliation. The specific aspiration, frustration, and reconciliation change to the surroundings, but will always be part of the mix of the journalism culture, of what it means to be a journalist.

Future Studies

It has been five years since the fieldwork, and the biggest change that has taken place in China is the administration. Hu Jintao and Wen Jiabao were the top leaders at the time of my fieldwork; they were succeeded by Xi Jinping and Li Keqiang in 2013. The media environment has yet again changed with more nuanced and tighter control, indicated by the trend of cracking down on journalists and news organizations not for what they report and publish, but for other reasons like financial misconduct.

In September 2014, executives and editors of 21st Century Net (21cbh. com) and its affiliated *21st Century Business Herald* newspaper were detained for alleged extortion (Zheng, 2014; Zhou & Yan, 2014). The authorities said the website threatened companies planning for an initial public offering with negative coverage and forced these companies to sign multimillion-dollar advertisement deals (Mi, 2015; Zhou, 2014). Shen Hao, founder and editor-in-chief of *21st Century Business Herald*, which ran the website, was sentenced to four years in jail (Mi, 2015).

On the surface, this case is simply law enforcement doing their job, as the authorities have always taken a stand against journalists extorting their sources for monetary gains (Spegele & Chen, 2014; Zheng, 2014; Zhou & Yan, 2014). Looking deeper, however, the case has more to it. Shen Hao is a well-known, prominent journalist in China who gained his fame as a talented and courageous journalist while working for the *Southern Weekend*, a newspaper with a reputation of speaking against the authorities. The parent company of the *Business Herald* and *Southern Weekend* is the Southern Daily Group, which "for many years has dared to speak up" (Zheng, 2014, para. 3). The true motivation was interpreted by some critics as to "kill the chicken and scare the monkey" (Zheng, 2014, para. 1), a Chinese saying meaning punishing somebody in order to intimidate someone else who has close relationship with the punished.

The arrests and sentencing of journalists from the 21st Century company, together with other similar cases where journalists were taken away by police for charges of bribery, extortion, or buying a prostitute, were also seen as "part of the general crackdown and tightening of freedom of speech. It's just that they are picking on the obvious wrongdoers first," a source was quoted by the *South China Morning Post* as saying (Zou & Lau, 2014).

Another controlling measure implemented by the new administration was cracking down on social media, especially in the name of clearing rumors and lies. Around the same time of the arrests at the 21st Century media company, the authorities waged a nationwide campaign against "rumor-mongers" on the Internet, especially social media platforms like Weibo. As a result, many opinion leaders on Weibo, people who have millions of followers, posted less frequently and carried out self-censorship to delete some previous postings. The antirumor campaign had a chilling effect on social media and likely functioned to silence dissenting voices (Boehler, 2013).

Under such circumstances, the question arises whether journalists' aspirations will yield to the political pressure. If not, it can be speculated that there will be even more frustration and tension. But this requires a different study to explore how journalism culture is shifting under the new administration.

In addition, the usefulness of the aspiration-frustration-reconciliation model can be tested by applying it to other groups of journalists. The model can be used as an analytical framework to conduct cultural inquiries, or it can be quantified into measurable variables to evaluate the variation among different journalists in terms of their perceived level of frustration. It is my hope that the current study and the theoretical framework derived from it can provide a useful framework for a more holistic and systematic probe of journalism culture of different groups of journalists in different news organizations, societies, and cultures.

References

Berkowitz, D. (2011). Introduction: From sociological roots to cultural perspectives. In D. Berkowitz (Ed.), *Cultural meaning of news* (pp. xi–xxii). Thousand Oaks, CA: Sage.

Boehler, P. (2013, September 13). Silencing Weibo's voices of dissent? *South China Morning Post.*

Burgh, H. D. (2003). *The Chinese journalist: Mediating information in the world's most populous country.* London, New York: RoutledgeCurzon.

Cheek, T. (1997). *Propaganda and culture in Mao's China: Deng Tuo and the intelligentsia.* Broadbridge, UK: Clarendon Press.

Gans, H. J. (1979). *Deciding what's news: A study of CBS Evening News, NBC Nightly News, Newsweek, and Time.* New York: Pantheon Books.

He, Z. (2000). Chinese communist party press in a tug-of-war: A political-economy analysis of the *Shenzhen Special Zone Daily.* In C. Lee (Ed.), *Power, money, and media: Communication patterns and bureaucratic control in cultural China* (pp. 112–151). Evanston, IL: Northwestern University Press.

He, Z. (2003). How do the Chinese media reduce organizational incongruence? Bureaucratic capitalism in the name of communism. In C. Lee (Ed.), *Chinese media, global contexts* (pp. 196–214). London: Routledge.

Hsiao, C., & Yang, M. (1990). "Don't force us to lie": The case of the *world economic herald.* In C. Lee (Ed.), *Voices of China: The interplay of politics and journalism* (pp. 111–121). New York: Guilford Press.

Larson, C. (2011, January 29). The plight of the Chinese newspaper reporter. *The Atlantic.*

Lynch, D. C. (1999). *After the propaganda state: Media, politics, and "thought work" in reformed China.* Stanford, CA: Stanford University Press.

Mi, Y. (2015). 21世紀報系沈顥獲刑 中國媒體報道受限 [*Shen Hao of the 21st century newspaper sentenced; Chinese media limited in reporting the incident*]. Retrieved May 4, 2016, from http://www.bbc.com/zhongwen/trad/china/2015/12/151224_china_media_boss_sentenced

Pan, Z. (2000). Improving reform activities: The changing reality of journalistic practice in China. In C. Lee (Ed.), *Power, money, and media: Communication patterns and bureaucratic control in cultural China* (pp. 68–111). Evanston, IL: Northwestern University Press.

Pan, Z., & Lu, Y. (2003). Localizing professionalism: Discursive practices in China's media reforms. In C. Lee (Ed.), *Chinese media, global contexts* (pp. 215–236). London: Routledge.

Polumbaum, J. (1990). The tribulations of China's journalists after a decade of reform. In C. Lee (Ed.), *Voices of China: The interplay of politics and journalism* (pp. 33–68). New York: Guilford Press.

Polumbaum, J. (2008). *China ink: The changing face of Chinese journalism.* Lanham, MD: Rowman & Littlefield.

Reese, S. D. (2001). Understanding the global journalist: A hierarchy-of-influences approach. *Journalism Studies, 2*(2), 173–187. doi: 10.1080/14616700120042060

Schudson, M. (1997/1989). The sociology of news production. In D. Berkowitz (Ed.), *Social meaning of news* (pp. 7–22). Thousand Oaks, CA: Sage.

Shoemaker, P. J., & Vos, T. P. (2009). *Gatekeeping theory.* London, New York: Routledge.

Spegele, B., & Chen, T. (2014, September 26). China increases scrutiny of business journalists. *Wall Street Journal.*

Zha, J. (1995). *China pop: How soap operas, tabloids, and bestsellers are transforming a culture.* New York: New Press.

Zheng, H. (2014). 港媒透露"21世纪网" 遭整肃祸起新年献词一役 [*Hong Kong media reveal that 21st Century Net cracked down due to fight over New Year editorial*]. Retrieved May 4, 2016, from http://cn.rfi.fr

Zhou, L. (2014, September 11). News website chiefs detail extortion scheme. *The South China Morning Post.*

Zhou, L., & Yan, A. (2014, September 04). 8 news, PR staff held in blackmail inquiry. *South China Morning Post.*

Zuo, M., & Lau, M. (2014, September 25). Police take away top media executives. *South China Morning Post.*

Index